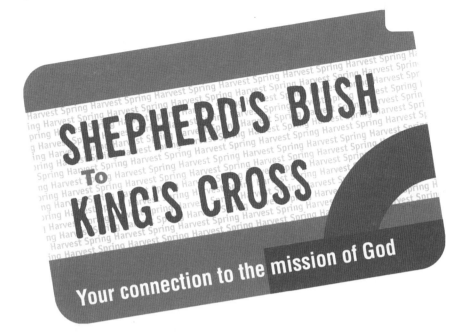

SHEPHERD'S BUSH
To
KING'S CROSS

Your connection to the mission of God

Spring Harvest 2003

Study Guide
by Gerard Kelly

Equipping the Church for action

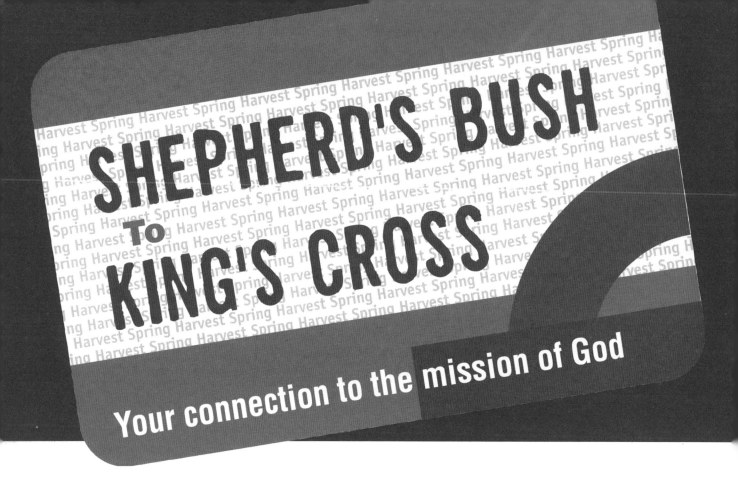

SHEPHERD'S BUSH To KING'S CROSS

Your connection to the mission of God

1 DESTINATIONS AND DEFINITIONS
Mission

mission *noun* **1** a purpose for which a person or group of people is sent. **2 a** a journey made for a scientific, military or religious purpose; **b** a group of people sent on such a journey. **3** a flight with a specific purpose, such as a bombing raid or a task assigned to the crew of a spacecraft. **4** a group of people sent somewhere to have discussions, especially political ones. **5** (*usually* **mission in life**) someone's chosen, designated or assumed purpose in life or vocation. **6 a** a group of missionaries; **b** the building occupied by them. **7** a centre run by a charitable or religious organisation, etc to provide a particular service in the community. Also *as adj • mission control*.
ETYMOLOGY: 16c: from Latin *missionis*, from *mittere* to send.

Missio Dei [mission of God] *noun* **1** all of the above, applied to God.
ETYMOLOGY: 20c: from Latin *missio*, MISSION, *dei*, OF GOD.

GOD HEARS

GOD DELIVERS

GOD CARES

GOD RULES

What this Guide is

This Study Guide forms the basis of the teaching at Spring Harvest 2003, but can equally be used in other contexts. Its theme is the Mission of God in the light of:

- The call of Moses and the Exodus story
- The death and resurrection of Jesus
- The challenges facing the Christian church
- The need for each believer to connect with God's mission

The Study Guide is arranged in four sections, each of which deals with two themes. At the Spring Harvest Main Event, these relate to days 2 to 5 of the programme, but in other contexts they can be dealt with differently – whether in sequence or not.

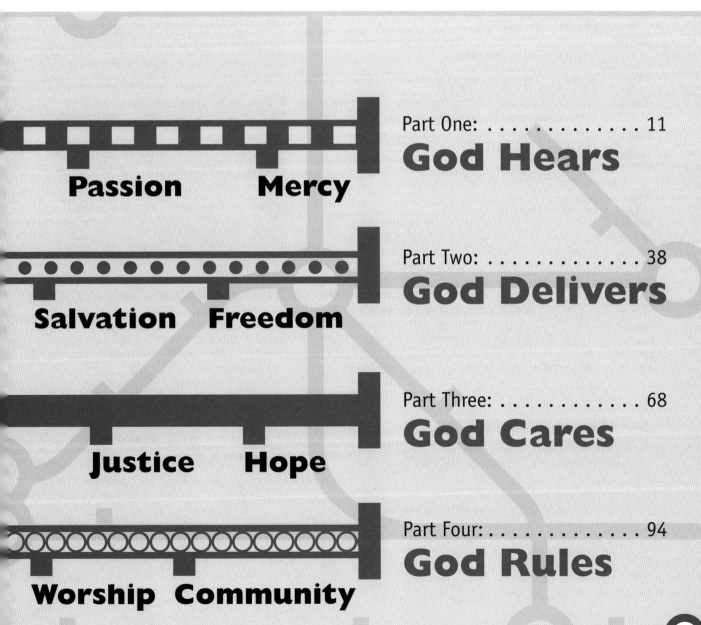

The Study Guide is laid out to give the maximum degree of flexibility in the way it is used and applied. Even though our titles hint at route-maps and set journeys, there are actually any number of routes through this material. For group study – including the teaching Zones at the Spring Harvest Main Event – the intention is that group leaders should select a range of items from the menu of each theme and link them together. For the individual reader, it is possible to work through the entire Study Guide systematically. Either way, your journey will be made up of the following key elements for each of the eight themes:

Destinations and Definitions
A brief introduction to the theme.

District Lines
Exploring the theme in the immediate context of the Exodus narrative. What can we learn from the history and experiences of the Hebrew slaves?

Main Lines
Exploring the theme in the light of
● 　the wider biblical record
● 　the life, death and resurrection of Jesus
● 　the challenges facing the Christian church.

Branch Lines
Drawing out secondary issues that arise from the consideration of this theme.

Fellow Travellers
Longer quotes and extracts from writers who have themselves considered and explored this theme.

Applications
Suggestions as to how and where the exploration of this theme might be applied.

Connections
Extracts from the 'Connect' Bible Studies published by The Damaris Trust, Scripture Union and Premier Radio, linking the theme to the products of today's popular culture. Connect Bible Studies are written to help groups dig into their Bibles, and get to know them better. They also help people think through topical issues in a biblical way, which is why they are based on popular films or books. A summary is provided for people who haven't watched the film or read the book. Each study runs for four weeks, and is available on the internet and from Christian bookshops. Use the books to stimulate thought and discussion in a biblical context. Tailor them to your group by selecting from the

The Book Stall
Alongside each theme, we will recommend books and other resources to help your further exploration of the themes we have explored, indicating:

Leadership Titles:
Recommended for leaders, preachers and teachers and for those wanting to take a more in-depth look at the material we have covered and its sources.

Mainstream Titles:
Recommended for adult readership – these are books that take a broad look at key aspects of the themes covered.

Specialised Titles:
These are books that take a closer look at a particular area alluded to in the Study Guide material. Recommended for those with a special interest in the area covered.

In addition, two other icons will appear from time to time in the text. These are:

Close Up:
Indicating comments and observations that home in on a particular aspect of the material, but are not central to the Main Line, Branch Line or District Line in question.

In Brief:
Indicating short paragraphs or quotations that sum up in a few words the thrust of a particular section of the material.

wide range of options and approaches to the material. Discover what the Bible says about issues raised by popular books, films, television programmes and songs.■

Bible Readings
How do you hide from God?

It may sound a strange question but our Bible Readings this week tell the story of someone who tried to do it – and failed.

Jonah was invited to get involved in the Mission of God – and he turned the offer down. Loudly.

So loudly in fact that he ran as fast as he could in the opposite direction. This is odd when we consider all that Jonah had going for him:

● 　A firm faith

● 　A call to be a prophet
● 　An understanding of God
● 　A track record of faithful following
● 　An awareness of the needs of his world

But when God called, Jonah didn't want to know. The Mission of God didn't fit in with the mission of Jonah.

Our Bible Readings each morning take us with Jonah as he discovers (the hard way) that, when it comes to dealing with God, obedience is always the best response.

And – who knows – while studying Jonah's story, we may catch ourselves looking in the mirror.

WHY EXODUS?

We are exploring the book of Exodus because it contributes foundational ideas for an understanding of the Mission of God. It is not the only biblical source on God's mission, and neither does it tell the whole story: but it is a rich and dramatic account of God's dealings with humanity, and as such has plenty to teach us. We approach the text as Christians, not as Jews: so we will frequently refer to the meaning of the text in the light of Christ. In its original form and context, Exodus is a Hebrew story: but we also read it as a profoundly Christian text. ■

Before departure, four comments on the overall flavour of the journey

WHY THESE EIGHT THEMES?

The eight themes chosen do not lay claim to being a comprehensive 'menu' of the Mission of God. When you take a journey from Shepherd's Bush to King's Cross, the first thing you realise is how wide God's mission is. There really isn't anything outside its scope, so no list of eight words will ever do it justice. The eight themes we have chosen, though, do begin to give a flavour of the breadth and majesty of God's mission. We have selected them because they are important aspects of the Mission of God, and because:

● **They all pass through Shepherd's Bush.**
Each of these eight themes is present and evident in the call of Moses and the subsequent events of the Exodus.

● **They all take you to King's Cross.**
Each of these eight themes is also clearly present and evident in the life, death and resurrection of Jesus.

● **They all call at your home address.**
Each of these eight themes is relevant to the lives we lead in the contemporary world: not just for the leaders of churches and the strategists of mission, but for all of us as we work, rest and play in the light of God.

Each of the eight is a thread or a colour that runs through the whole of the Exodus narrative – and through biblical and church history. ■

WHY THE MISSION OF GOD?

We have come to this theme with a strong sense of God's timing and direction. Our prayer is that individuals, families and churches, through their engagement with this material, will discover anew the passion and purpose of joining God in his mission. It is our conviction that there is no higher calling or vocation than to 'connect' with God's mission – in the ways that he has planned and prepared for each of us. It's his mission – but every one of us has a part in it. ■

Part One:

GOD HEARS
PASSION & MERCY

Bible Reading, Jonah 1:1-17

¹The word of the LORD came to Jonah son of Amittai: ²"Go to the great city of Nineveh and preach against it, because its wickedness has come up before me."

³But Jonah ran away from the LORD and headed for Tarshish. He went down to Joppa, where he found a ship bound for that port. After paying the fare, he went aboard and sailed for Tarshish to flee from the LORD.

⁴Then the LORD sent a great wind on the sea, and such a violent storm arose that the ship threatened to break up. ⁵All the sailors were afraid and each cried out to his own god. And they threw the cargo into the sea to lighten the ship.

But Jonah had gone below deck, where he lay down and fell into a deep sleep. ⁶The captain went to him and said, "How can you sleep? Get up and call on your god! Maybe he will take notice of us, and we will not perish."

⁷Then the sailors said to each other, "Come, let us cast lots to find out who is responsible for this calamity." They cast lots and the lot fell on Jonah.

⁸So they asked him, "Tell us, who is responsible for making all this trouble for us? What do you do? Where do you come from? What is your country? From what people are you?"

⁹He answered, "I am a Hebrew and I worship the LORD, the God of heaven, who made the sea and the land."

¹⁰This terrified them and they asked, "What have you done?" (They knew he was running away from the LORD, because he had already told them so.)

¹¹The sea was getting rougher and rougher. So they asked him, "What should we do to you to make the sea calm down for us?"

¹²"Pick me up and throw me into the sea," he replied, "and it will become calm. I know that it is my fault that this great storm has come upon you."

¹³Instead, the men did their best to row back to land. But they could not, for the sea grew even wilder than before. ¹⁴Then they cried to the LORD, "O LORD, please do not let us die for taking this man's life. Do not hold us accountable for killing an innocent man, for you, O LORD, have done as you pleased." ¹⁵Then they took Jonah and threw him overboard, and the raging sea grew calm. ¹⁶At this the men greatly feared the LORD, and they offered a sacrifice to the LORD and made vows to him.

¹⁷But the LORD provided a great fish to swallow Jonah, and Jonah was inside the fish three days and three nights.

Overview

God calls his spokesman, Jonah, to speak out against the evils found in Nineveh – capital of the powerful Assyrian empire. But Jonah refuses to get involved in the *Mission of God* and runs away.

His disobedience leads to disaster for Jonah and others who suffer the consequences.

But the chapter ends on a brighter note. The Lord doesn't write Jonah off. He provides a way of escape – a most unlikely route to a new beginning. We face two important questions –
   Am I in the place God wants me to be?
   Am I doing what he has called me to do?

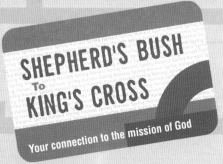

SHEPHERD'S BUSH
To
KING'S CROSS
Your connection to the mission of God

NOTES

PASSION

NOTES

> **Exodus 3:7–10**
> [7]The Lord said, "I have indeed seen the misery of my people in Egypt. I have heard them crying out because of their slave drivers, and I am concerned about their suffering. [8]So I have come down to rescue them from the hand of the Egyptians and to bring them up out of that land into a good and spacious land, a land flowing with milk and honey – the home of the Canaanites, Hittites, Amorites, Perizzites, Hivites and Jebusites. [9]And now the cry of the Israelites has reached me, and I have seen the way the Egyptians are oppressing them. [10]So now, go. I am sending you to Pharaoh to bring my people the Israelites out of Egypt."

Introduction

'As a boy growing up in the city, it was somewhat dangerous for me to walk to school all by myself. So my mother paid Harriet, a neighbourhood girl a few years older than I, to be responsible for getting me to and from school each day. Harriet was paid five cents a day for this service.

'As I grew older, I became very conscious of what I believed was an enormous amount of money going into Harriet's hands. So I went to my mother and told her that there was no need for her to pay Harriet any longer, that she should give me the nickel each day, and I would walk myself to school. I kept on begging and begging until my mother gave in and said, "Okay! If you're very careful, I'll give you the nickel a day, and you put the money in the bank and save it to buy Christmas presents for your sisters."

'That seemed like a good idea. So from that time on I walked myself to school, collected the money, and did not allow the Campolo wealth to leave the household. Years later, when my mother had passed on, I was at a family get-together with my sisters and I reminded them of my independent spirit even when I was a child... how I walked myself to school ... and how that translated into good presents for them at Christmas time.

'My sisters laughed at me and one of them said, 'Did you think that you went to school alone and came home alone? Every day when you left the house Mom followed you. And when you came out of school at the end of the day, she was there. She always made sure that you didn't notice her, but she watched over you coming and going, just to make sure you were safe and that nobody hurt you... she would follow you home then sneak in the back door... she had been watching over you all the time.'
Tony Campolo
[Let Me Tell You A Story, Word Publishing Group, 2000]

This fragment from an urban childhood is separated by thousands of miles, countless generations, and massive cultural differences from the story of Moses – and yet it parallels the discoveries the old shepherd makes. Arrested by the curious sign of a bush that burns but is not consumed, Moses finds himself drawn into an encounter with Yahweh – the God of his fathers. In this encounter, he receives surprising news. Where he might have believed that God was distant and silent, uninterested in the plight of the Hebrew slaves, he finds the opposite to be true. God is there: he has been watching over his people. He has heard their cry, is moved by their plight and in mercy he determines to act for their salvation. Moses discovers that this Yahweh God:

- Has heard the cry of the Hebrew slaves
- Has remembered his people and his promise
- Has seen the reality of their slavery
- Knows the depth of their plight

Far from being passive and unmoved, God is active and responsive, and has never abandoned the promises he made to Moses' ancestors. The Exodus adventure begins with this discovery that God is indeed with his people: that he has never ceased to watch over them and that his promises and plan have not been abandoned. He is passionate about them, and his passion will be expressed in mercy towards them.

If our understanding of the mission of God is to be shaped by this unique, foundational story, then we too must recognise that mission *is grounded in the passion of God and finds expression in his mercy.* ■

PASSION

1. DESTINATIONS AND DEFINITIONS
Passion

passion *noun* **1** a violent emotion, eg hate, anger or envy.
2 a fit of anger. **3** sexual love or desire. **4 a** an enthusiasm
• *has a passion for bikes*; **b** something for which one has
great enthusiasm • *Bikes are his passion.* **5** martyrdom.
ETYMOLOGY: 12c: French, from Latin *passio*, from *pati* to
suffer.

Passion *noun* **1** (*usually* **the Passion**) the suffering and
death of Christ. **2** an account of this from one of the
Gospels. **3** a musical setting of one of these accounts.

© Copyright Chambers Harrap Publishers Ltd 2002

God is passionate about the future he has for his people,
and will act for their liberation and salvation. Exodus is
a story of passion...

2. DISTRICT LINE
Passion at Shepherd's Bush

Exodus 2:23–25

*²³During that long period, the king of Egypt died. The
Israelites groaned in their slavery and cried out, and
their cry for help because of their slavery went up to
God. ²⁴God heard their groaning and he remembered his
covenant with Abraham, with Isaac and with Jacob. ²⁵So
God looked on the Israelites and was concerned about
them.*

The narrative has already told us something of the
passion of Moses – his misguided attempts to intervene
on behalf of the Hebrews have lead to violence, murder
and exile. In due course these passions, transformed by
the power of God, will play their part in the story. But
Exodus 2:23–25 makes it clear that the encounter at the
burning bush is not grounded in the passion of Moses,
but in that of God himself. These verses introduce God's
encounter with Moses and use four consecutive verbs to
describe God's actions: God heard, God remembered, God
looked (= considered), and God knew (= was concerned).

The divine initiative in appearing to Moses is seen as
the direct outworking of these four actions.

*'Mission does not originate with human sources for
ultimately it is not a human enterprise. Mission is rooted
in the nature of God, who sends and saves.'*
Gailyn Van Rheenen
[*Missions: Biblical Foundations and Contemporary Strategies*, p14]

● God hears

The misery of the slaves is expressed in their groaning
and crying: but there is no evidence that this cry is
directed to their God. Their surprise and unbelief when
God, through Moses, answers seem to indicate a cry not
of prayer but of pain. In their plight they cry out – not
knowing who might hear. But God does hear. Their cry
'goes up to God' and reaches him – because he is watching over his people. He hears because he is present with
them. Though they fear that their groaning has echoed
in an empty universe, with no source of rescue to be
found, the creator God, who made promises to their
fathers long ago, has heard them. ■

● God remembers

*'Most reassuring of all is the fact that God remembers.
What he had promised some four hundred to six hundred
years earlier to Abraham, Isaac, and Jacob, he began
to bring to fruition as Israel left Egypt for the Land of
Promise. The covenant at Sinai was but another step in
God's fulfillment of his promise to the patriarchs.'*
[*Expository Bible Commentary*]

The remembering of God is a cornerstone of his passion and response. The book of Exodus does not exist
in isolation, nor is it the beginning of the story. Its
opening words "and these are the names of..." link the
narrative to that of Genesis, and its first seven verses
are "a virtual commentary on the ancient promise made
to Abraham, Isaac, and Jacob that their seed would be

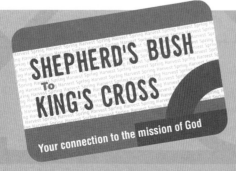

*'The Spirit of Christ is the spirit of
missions, and the nearer we get to
him the more intensely missionary
we must become.'*
Henry Martyn

Close Up:

Abraham Kuyper claimed that 'all mission flows from God's sovereignty, not from God's love or compassion'. This is not a suggestion that God has no compassion, but that before compassion comes into play there stand the promises and purposes of God: the good plans for the creation that are sealed in covenant and immovable for all time. Even if there had been no slavery, and no groaning, God's commitment to his promise-plan would be unchanged. The God who responds to the people's cry is the God who has already determined, beyond space and time, to bless them.

as numerous as the stars of heaven and the sands of the sea (e.g., Gen 15:5; 22:17)."

[*Expository Bible Commentary*]

This is the continuing story of the promise-plan of God: the outworking of the Genesis covenants. When Yahweh announces himself to Moses as 'the God of your father, the God of Abraham, the God of Isaac and the God of Jacob', he leaves no room for doubt that he is the covenant God: the God who in ages past made startling promises to the Hebrew fathers. His response to the groaning of the slaves is not only a stirring of compassion: it is also a remembering of his promise. ■

Close Up:

God's remembering is not simply a passive, mental recollection, but leads seamlessly to action. In Genesis 8:1 we are told that God 'remembered' Noah and his family shut away in the ark – and in his remembering 'he sent a wind over the earth, and the waters receded.' In 1 Samuel 1:19 God 'remembers' the childless Hannah, and as a result 'in the course of time Hannah conceived and gave birth to a son.' Where God is described as 'remembering' his covenant, his remembering is always associated with, and seen in, his activity.

● **God sees**

'Israel's God is not an abstract principle behind the universe, nor a distant ruler interfering occasionally in human affairs. He is a person who makes himself known, makes himself vulnerable and commits himself faithfully to those who trust him.'
Stephen Travis
[*The Bible as a Whole*, p47]

Four times in chapters 3 and 4 of Exodus, we are told that God has seen the sufferings of his people. This becomes foundational to the unfolding of the story when it is the key that unlocks the reluctance of the Hebrews to believe Moses. In 4:31, it is when the slaves finally realise that God has seen their misery and is concerned about them that they believe. The implication is of a seeing that goes beyond mere sight and awareness. The 'seeing' of the all-seeing God would naturally include all that had come to pass in Egypt. In an objective sense, God sees the plight of the slaves because there is nothing that God does not see. But God's 'looking' here goes further: it implies consideration: he has seen and understood. He has taken account of the sufferings of his people.

Imagine a great crowd of refugees waiting at an immigration checkpoint to be admitted to a place of safety. They are tired, hungry and in need, each waiting for their case to be heard. In the sense that the crowd is visible to all, they have been seen: but if you asked each one 'have you been seen yet?' they would assume a different meaning. Moses was able to convince the Hebrew slaves that they had been 'seen' in this deeper

'First think WOW with God for missions. The HOW will follow. Never think HOW before WOW.'
Dan and Dave Davidson

PASSION

sense: that their case had been heard, and the greatest advocate in the universe was now fighting for them. ■

● God knows

Finally, God 'knew' or 'was concerned for' the sufferings of his people. His hearing, remembering and seeing has drawn him into their predicament. It cannot remain as knowledge only, but becomes a sharing of the predicament itself.

'For God to 'know' the people's sufferings testifies to God's experience of this suffering, indeed God's intimate experience. God is here depicted as one who is intimately involved in the suffering of the people. God has so entered into their sufferings as to have deeply felt what they are having to endure. God has chosen not to remain safe and secure in some heavenly abode, untouched by the sorrows of the world. God is not portrayed as a typical monarch dealing with the issue through subordinates or at some distance. God does not look at the suffering from the outside as through a window; God knows it from the inside.'
Terence E. Fretheim

[*Interpretation: Exodus*, p59–60]

Like God's 'seeing', his 'knowing' goes beyond the sense of 'knowing all things'. God chooses to take his knowledge of his people beyond mere empirical or statistical awareness. The awareness is inevitable to the all-knowing God: but this deeper involvement is his choice.

In Brief:

Moses encounters a God who has forgotten neither his people nor his promises – a God who is prepared to identify with and enter into the plight of a slave people. Whatever else emerges in the Exodus story and beyond, it begins with and is grounded in this revelation of the passion of God.

Imagine an Oscar ceremony in which the book of Exodus is featured as Best Film. If Moses were up for an award, what would it be? It must be that of Best Supporting Actor. The award for Best Actor could only go to the principal character, the one around whom the story turns: Yahweh, the Creator God. This is not the story of the Prince of Egypt: it is the story of the King of Heaven. ■

*'God heard
God remembered
God saw
God knew'*
Terence E. Fretheim

[*Interpretation: Exodus*, p48]

Main Lines

This four-fold expression of the passion of God provides a strong foundation for an understanding of Christian mission. It tells us that mission:

- **Is grounded in Passionate Love**: it begins with the *Missio Dei*, the Mission of God
- **Is expressed in Incarnate Love**: the ultimate expression of 'God with us'
- **Calls us to an Active Love**: we are invited to participate in God's passion

MAIN LINE
Missio Dei

'Missio Dei enunciates the good news that God is a God-for-people.'
David Bosch
'In the eternal and original sense, mission is missio Dei – God's sending.'
Timothy Yates

[*Mission: An Invitation To God's Future*, p29]

Catholic missionary Vincent Donovan tells of a significant breakthrough with one particular young tribesman, a leader of prayer and festivals among his people. He seemed a born religious leader, and once spent three

SHEPHERD'S BUSH
To
KING'S CROSS
Your connection to the mission of God

'Unbelief says: Some other time, but not now; some other place, but not here; some other people, but not us. Faith says: Anything he did anywhere else he will do here; anything he did any other time he is willing to do now; anything he ever did for other people he is willing to do for us!'
A W Tozer

days lying on the rim of an active volcano, searching with longing for God. But he did not see him. He had to return, to more prayers, more pleading. Then Donovan met him and said, 'You think you have been searching for God, Ole Sikii, as a lion hunts its prey; but no, it is God who has been seeking you – God sent me to you. God is here and has found you. You are not the lion hunting: God is the lion.'

While the religious history of humanity is largely the story of men and women seeking God, the Bible speaks movingly of a God who seeks out men and women. The foundational truth of Moses' Shepherd's Bush encounter is that God is the lion – it is he who reaches out to us.

Theologians capture this sense of God himself as the missionary in the term *missio Dei*: the mission of God. This is an affirmation that before the church, or individual Christians, can be in any sense 'missionary', God is himself a missionary God – and that any truly Christian mission is a reflection of, and participation in, the mission of God. Moses is not asked to initiate or deliver the liberation of the Hebrew slaves: he is asked to co-operate with the God who has already determined to do so. It is God who will act for the salvation of his people.

"God is the chief actor in this narrative," Stephen Travis affirms. "He plans a route for the journey back to Canaan (13:17–18). He leads and guides the people (13:18, 21). He intensifies the hardening of Pharaoh's heart so that his plans to prevent the Israelites' escape issue in self-destruction (14:4). He opens the way miraculously for Moses and the people to flee to safety. ... God works the miracle of the exodus through a human leader who is in tune with his plan, through a natural phenomenon (v. 21), and through the walk of faith across the temporarily dry land... God has acted in history to accomplish his purpose for the world."
[*The Bible as a whole*, pp48, 49]

This is not an isolated concept present only in the Exodus narrative – it is a foundational statement of the nature of God, evident from Genesis to Revelation.

"When Adam and Eve acquiesced to Satan's temptation in the Garden of Eden," Gailyn Van Rheenen writes, "God came searching for them, calling, 'Where are you?' This question testifies to the nature of God throughout all generations. ... He is always giving, relating, reconciling, redeeming!"
[*Missions: Biblical Foundations and Contemporary Strategies*, Zondervan, 1996, p14]

There are a number of significant implications in this assertion that the mission is not ours but God's: shaping our understanding of mission as a whole, and of our part in it.

◆ The Missio Dei reflects the nature of the three-in-one God: it is the mission of the Father, Son and Holy Spirit

The understanding of God as three-in-one is a cornerstone of the *missio Dei*. The mission of God is an extension of the self-giving, relational love that already exists within the Trinity.

Rose Dowsett writes: "The love that perfectly and mutually flows between the three persons of the Trinity – between Father, Son and Holy Spirit – must also spill over into love for human beings made by God. It is for this reason that immediately following the catastrophic disobedience of Adam and Eve, the Lord comes looking for them. Here is the missionary God in action himself, looking for the lost!"
[*The Great Commission*, p36]

Bryant L Myers asserts that it is only by this understanding that we can make sense of the world we live in: "What God is doing is also expressed in a Trinitarian formulation: God is saving the world through Christ in the power of the Holy Spirit. The question of who God is in an unjust and violent world can only be answered adequately by talking about what God is doing: saving a fallen and failed world in a particular way."
[*Walking with the Poor*, p24]

'Lord grant me ... that my lamp may feel thy kindling touch and know no quenching; may burn for me and for others may give light.'
Prayer of Columbanus

PASSION

◆ The church is called not to initiate and lead mission, but to follow the missionary God

'Mission is ultimately God's and we cannot determine how the Spirit may work, but rather we need to follow the Spirit's lead always in the hope of the change our God can and will bring.'

Andrew Lord

[*Spirit, Kingdom and Mission: A Charismatic Missiology*, p11]

Just as Moses was not asked to initiate mission but to follow the lead of the initiative-taking God, so the church does not lead in mission, but follows.

◆ The mission of God is the 'big picture' running through the Bible

The mission of God is the thread that runs through the very fabric of the biblical narrative from beginning to end. The God of redemption is the God of creation, who called the cosmos into being in Genesis and promises its final renewal in Revelation.

In *Salvation to the Ends of the Earth*, Andreas J. Köstenberger & Peter T. O'Brien affirm that the mission of God is the key by which the whole narrative of Scripture holds together:

'... the divine plan of extending salvation to the ends of the earth is the major thrust of the Scriptures from beginning to end. If the first indications of God's purposes for the world appear in the creation account of Genesis 1, and subsequently in the call of Abram (Gen 12) which is profoundly related to God's dealings with the nations, then the Bible ends with a vision of 'a great multitude that no-one could count, from every nation, tribe, people and language, standing before the throne and in front of the Lamb' praising in a loud voice and saying 'salvation belongs to our God, who sits on the throne, and to the Lamb' (Rev 7:9–10; cf. 14:6). God's saving plan for the

whole world forms a grand frame around the entire story of Scripture.'

[*Salvation to the Ends of the Earth*, p262]

Close Up:

David Howard, a former director of the Urbana missions convention in the USA, warns of the dangers of seeing Christian mission too narrowly, as simply a response to 'the Great Commission', rather than as the outworking of the character of God:

'The missionary enterprise of the church is not a pyramid built upside down with its point on one isolated text in the New Testament out of which we have built a huge structure known as missions. Rather, the missionary enterprise of the church is a great pyramid built right side up with its base running from Genesis 1 to Revelation 22. All of Scripture forms the foundation for the outreach of the gospel to the whole world.

[Quoted in Paul Borthwick – *Mission, God's Heart for the World*, p6]

Whatever role each Christian may be called upon to play in the mission of God (the 'micro' perspective) it will always be in keeping with the big picture of God's promise-plan for his creation (the 'macro' perspective). Moses was challenged to become one link in a chain – just as you or I will be challenged to be another – but in every case the chain itself begins with the creation of the world and will not end until the heavens and earth are renewed. For many Christians, the recovery of this 'big picture' of the plans of God will be the key to a deeper, more challenging and more fruitful grasp of their own place in mission.

The second foundational truth revealed in the Exodus narrative concerns the nature of God's love for us. If mission is rooted and grounded in the *missio Dei* – in God's initiative – it is sustained and driven by the passion of God's heart for his creatures.

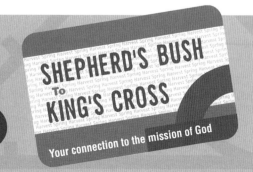

SHEPHERD'S BUSH
To
KING'S CROSS

Your connection to the mission of God

'Let our hearts beat with love of God. Let our passion spring from the character of God who owns and runs the world, who in his love and mercy chose us and brought us to himself, so that we may bring the compassion of our Lord Jesus Christ to our needy world. Thus shall we do what the Lord our God asks of us: to fear him, to walk in his way, to love him, to serve him, and to keep his commandments.'

Chris Wright

'God is passionate and intentional about pursuing lost people. He is deeply concerned to go after sinners and to bring them home into his arms of love.'
Mark Stibbe
[*Orphans to Heirs*, p12]

'The holy God enters into the suffering of the people and makes it his own (3:7). As in Hosea 11:9 and Isaiah 12:6, God is the Holy One in your midst.'
Terence E. Fretheim
[*Interpretation: Exodus*, p56]

MAIN LINE
Incarnate love

In the New Testament, these same ideas of God hearing, remembering, looking and knowing are linked to the birth of Jesus. There had been a similar 400-year period of apparent silence: but God has forgotten neither his people nor his promise. In Luke 1:46–55, Mary expresses the joy of the announced Incarnation in these terms, as does Zechariah, the father of John the Baptist, in Luke 1:67–79. Try reading these two songs of affirmation from Luke's Gospel in the light of all that we have seen of the God of the Exodus.

C S Lewis wrote: 'The central miracle asserted by Christians is the Incarnation. They say that God became man. Every other miracle prepares for this, or exhibits this, or results from this. Just as every natural event is the manifestation at a particular place and moment of nature's total character, so every particular Christian miracle manifests at a particular place and moment the character and significance of the Incarnation.'

Thus it is possible to look back to the 'I will be with you' of the burning bush and see it an expression of incarnation. Moses didn't know, and couldn't have known, how fully this Yahweh God would, in time, make good his promise to be with his creatures. Incarnation, in its full expression in Jesus, would have been so far beyond Moses' experience and understanding as to be incomprehensible in his time and context: but incarnation is present, in essence, in the promise of God. The important thing for Christian readers of the Exodus text to understand is that this Yahweh – the 'I will be with you' God – is the God made incarnate in Jesus, and that the Incarnation is the ultimate and complete expression of the passionate love of this same God.

Close Up:

Jurgen Moltmann movingly links this concept of a suffering God with much later Jewish experience, using an extract from a book written by a survivor of Auschwitz: 'The SS hanged two Jewish men and a youth in front of the whole camp. The men died quickly, but the death throes of the youth lasted for half an hour. "Where is God? Where is he?" someone asked behind me. As the youth still hung in torment in the noose after a long time, I heard the man call again, "Where is God now?" And I heard a voice in myself answer: "Where is he? He is here. He is hanging there on the gallows... ." Any other answer would be blasphemy,' Moltmann concludes. 'There cannot be any other Christian answer to the question of this torment.'

No fact more fully represents the passionate love of God than the fact of the Incarnation, in which God's willingness to enter into our suffering and condition is literally given flesh and blood. In Christ God not only takes on human flesh, but descends to the very deepest place of human suffering: becoming a slave to death itself.

'The fact that Christ entered into the depth of darkness on the cross,' Derek Tidball writes, 'means that he is able to identify sympathetically with the darkest of human situations. A God who remained majestically insulated in his heaven, impervious to our suffering, would not be a worthy or credible God in our suffering world.'
[*The Message of The Cross*, p147]

'His is not a slushy, naïve sentimentalism but a tangible, passionate and active love. That love is the lifeblood that he wants to put in our veins for the good of a needy, hurting world.'
Fran Beckett

PASSION

In Brief:

The passion of God finds expression in the Passion of Christ: the final answer to the question 'How far is God prepared to go to save us?'

'The Father's love for us is a love that costs, that hurts, that suffers. We need to remember that our adoption is free, but it is not cheap. It cost the Father dear to send his one and only Son, knowing we would reject, torture and kill him.'

Mark Stibbe

[*Orphans to Heirs – Celebrating our spiritual adoption*, p50]

MAIN LINE
Active love

vocation *noun* **1** a particular occupation or profession, especially one regarded as needing dedication and skill. **2** a feeling of being especially suited for a particular type of work. **3** *relig* a divine calling to adopt a religious life or perform good works. **vocational adj. vocationally adverb.** **ETYMOLOGY**: 15c: from Latin *vocare* to call.

We all have to find our place in the universe. This is what calling or vocation is all about. Here is how Os Guinness describes the feeling of finding a sense of vocation:

'I felt as though I was about to fill a space in the world that was meant for me and had long awaited me, a mould, as it were, made for me alone, but discerned by me only this very moment. I was a molten substance, impatient, unendurably impatient, to pour into my mould, to fill it full, without air bubbles or cracks, before I cooled and stiffened.'

Os Guinness

[*The Call*, Carlisle: Paternoster/Spring Harvest, 2001, p53]

Having established that all mission begins with the initiative of God and is grounded in the passion of God,

the Exodus narrative goes on to make clear that mission *involves the people of God*. If the first surprise for Moses is that the God he feared absent is present, active and ready to move, the second surprise is that he, Moses, has a role in God's plan. Whatever else was happening in the encounter at Shepherd's Bush, Moses was coming face to face with his calling – the purpose for which he had been prepared from birth, the means by which he would 'make a dent in the universe'. Not only has God been watching over the Hebrew slaves – he has also watched over the life of Moses. The passion of God becomes personal when Moses begins to see that he is being called to play a part.

It is all too easy, reading from our contemporary perspective, to think of Moses as a 'religious' leader, called to the spiritual task of leading God's people. But this is only part of the picture. In the course of pursuing God's call, Moses will develop as a politician and military strategist, as a judge and legal expert: as well as being an accomplished journalist, songwriter and worship leader! Calling is not about 'Christian ministry', but about 'living for the praise and glory of the Lord and serving God's purposes in every context of life.'

Jani Rubery

[*More Than A Job*, p34]

The call of Moses at the burning bush highlights several aspects of 'calling' and vocation:

◆ God's call is the highest call

Moses has struggled with his own confused identity and with his frustration at being unable to help the Hebrew slaves by his own efforts: but at the burning bush he receives a call from God that puts the struggles of his life into perspective and offers him a sense of purpose stronger than any he has known. In a sense nothing changes in Moses: he is the same person he was before the call – but in another sense everything is different, and he undergoes 'the most comprehensive reorientation and the most profound motivation in human experience.'

[*The Call*, p7]

SHEPHERD'S BUSH
To
KING'S CROSS

Your connection to the mission of God

'Once having the vision, the second step to holy obedience is this: Begin where you are. Obey now. Use what little obedience you are capable of, even if it be like a grain of mustard seed. Begin where you are.'

Thomas R. Kelly

In *Living on Purpose*, Tom and Christine Sine explore the difference this sense of calling can make in our lives.

"Purpose is that deepest dimension within us – our central core or essence – where we have a profound sense of who we are, where we came from, and where we are going," they write. "God is still inviting disciples to discover the difference their lives can make if they, like Jesus, make God's purposes their purposes."

[*Living on Purpose*, p11]

◆ The call of God takes account of our strengths and our weaknesses

In God's extended conversation with Moses, areas of both strength and weakness are touched upon. In one sense Moses is unfit for the task – an inadequacy he feels acutely. In another sense he is uniquely gifted for the role God has for him: no other Hebrew would have the access he can have to Pharaoh.

'God picks a known *entity... God's creative work in Moses' life to this point has shaped a human being with endowments suited to the tasks ahead.'*

Terence E. Fretheim

[*Interpretation: Exodus*, p56]

The call of God acknowledges, uses the strengths of Moses, and meets and compensates for his weaknesses. The shepherd's staff – a symbol not only of the ordinariness of Moses' life but also of his exile and failure – is transformed into the symbol of God's power.

◆ God works secretly in our lives to prepare us for the tasks he has for us

It becomes clear as Moses begins to consider the call of God that this same God has been silently at work in his life, preparing and refining him for the task. His natural intolerance of injustice has brought nothing but trouble, but will be one of the threads God is able to weave into a new plan.

'The very impulse that led Moses to avenge wrongdoing apart from due process of law was developed to do the work of God when God finished seasoning him through the experiences of life!'

[*Expository Bible Commentary*]

And the call is confirmed by the remarkable fact that Aaron "is already on his way" to meet his brother. "No sooner has God called Moses than he is at work through circumstances to make good the call."

◆ We are called to share in God's mission – and to share in his passion

Before the call of God, the passions of Moses are the root of his problems and the cause of his exile: he is too impetuous for his own good. But that does not imply that the Moses who emerges from the Shepherd's Bush encounter is in some way less passionate. Called by God, Moses discovers passions strong enough to sustain a protracted battle of wills with Pharaoh and deep enough that he will intercede before God for the forgiveness of the errant Hebrew people.

'Truth without emotion produces dead orthodoxy and a church full (or half-full) of artificial admirers (like people who write generic anniversary cards for a living). On the other hand, emotion without truth produces empty frenzy and cultivates shallow people who refuse the discipline of rigorous thought. ... Strong affections for God rooted in truth are the bone and marrow of biblical worship.'

John Piper

[*Desiring God*, p76]

Love is listening

'The simple truth is if we want people to listen to us, we have to listen to them first. People listen to people who listen.'

Bill Muir

[Three Story Evangelism]

PASSION

In Brief:

God does not need Moses in the way that a driver with a broken engine needs a man from the AA: God is quite capable of fulfilling his purposes by his own power and action. But he chooses to work with and through 'called' people.

BRANCH LINES
Open all hours?

A recent controversy in theological circles relates closely to this notion of God's passion and surrounds the idea of the 'openness' of God. 'Open theism' emphasises the depth at which God feels genuine emotion, and the sense that he is 'open to' the relationships he forms with his creatures.

'It would therefore seem that God, like us, is personal existence. If so, then God enjoys relationships, has feelings, makes decisions, formulates plans and acts to fulfil them.'
Clark Pinnock
[*The Openness of God*, p39]

Open theists emphasise the relational aspects of God's nature, looking to the living room rather than the courtroom for inspiration:

'The husband-wife and parent-child metaphors illuminate the experience of God in a unique and indispensable way. Whereas the metaphors of king and subject, judge and criminal emphasise power and punishment in God's relation to his people, these family metaphors emphasise love and commitment. "When God is portrayed as betrayed husband," one scholar observes, "then God's own frustrated desires and suffering are brought into focus."'
Clark Pinnock
[*The Openness of God*, p25, 24]

Particularly contentious is the implication that God does not know or foresee every detail of the future, but leaves much of it 'open', dependent on the free response of his creatures.

'To say that God is ignorant of future creaturely decisions is like saying that God is deaf to silence. It makes no sense, because before they exist such decisions are nothing for God to be ignorant of.'
Richard Rice
[Quoted in John Piper, *Tested by Fire*, p23]

This has led some to claim that open theism is a view that 'has never been embraced as part of orthodoxy by any major Christian body in the history of the Church.' [John Piper, *Tested by Fire*, p23], and that 'the fantasy that God is ignorant of the future is a heresy that must be rejected on scriptural grounds.' [Thomas Oden, cited in John Piper, *Tested by Fire*, p23] Does God already know what the future holds – and how each of us will respond to him – or does he remain 'open' to the different options that our different possible responses will produce?

In Brief:

It is all but impossible to reconcile these two opposing views: but there are important things here that need to be held in tension. Perhaps the resolution of the debate lies in the belief that the Glory of God is so great and his power so beyond us, that it is possible for both these ideas to be true – that he is at one and the same time the sovereign God who 'knows the end from the beginning' and the loving, responsive God who makes space in his plans for creaturely involvement. This at least seems to be the picture of God that emerges from the Exodus narrative, where both pictures are offered and no effort is made to reconcile them.

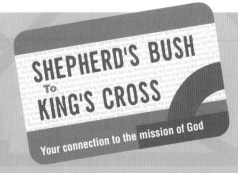

SHEPHERD'S BUSH
To
KING'S CROSS
Your connection to the mission of God

OPEN THEISM:
THE THEOLOGICAL DEBATE

Traditionally, theologians have argued that since God knows 'the end from the beginning' (Isa 46:10), he must be 'omniscient'. By this, they have understood that he knows everything that will happen.

Open theists continue to use the term 'omniscience', but deny that it need imply such exhaustive divine fore-knowledge. Indeed, they suggest that God deliberately eschews such knowledge because it would jeopardise the creative, reciprocal nature of his relationship with us. This relationship, they suggest, is one of dynamic mutual understanding and dialogue. "What kind of dialogue is it," Clark Pinnock asks, "where one party already knows what the other will say and do?"[1]

Open theists are keen to defend this position from Scripture. While acknowledging that God keeps the 'big picture' of redemption in view, they maintain he often regards the future conditionally rather than deterministically. He instructs Jeremiah to preach to the Israelites so they may listen, and suggests that if they do he may 'change' his 'mind' about the disaster he has 'intended to bring' (Jer 26:2–3). God 'relents' from his plan to destroy Nineveh (Jonah 3:10). He tests men and women, apparently to discover how they will react (Gen 22:12; Deut 8:2; 2 Chron 32:31). Even Jesus, who foretells his own death early on in his public ministry, still seems to recognise the possibility of escaping it in Gethsemane (Matt 26:39). Bearing such texts in mind, open theists add that their theology makes more sense of prayer. If God has fixed everything in advance, they claim, why is he so often swayed by the intercessions of his followers (e.g. Exod 32:14; Num 11: 1–2; Deut 9:13–14; 1 Chron 21:15)?

Traditionalists have retorted that the God of the Bible knows specific details of the future rather than merely broad themes. He enumerates the years of Israel's exiles (Gen 15:13–14; Jer 29:10–11). He names individuals before they are born, discloses biographies before they unfold, and schedules the fate of specific kingdoms (1 Kings 13:2-3; Isa 44:28; 45:1–6; Dan 2:31; Ezek 26:7–21).

In scores of prophecies, he describes the coming Messiah in startling detail. That Messiah, his Son Jesus, foretells Peter's denial, Judas' betrayal and the events of the last days (Matt 26:34; John 6:64–71; Matt 24–25). Only a God who knows this fully how things will turn out, say classical theists, can guarantee to accomplish his will (Job 42: 2; Rom 8:28; Eph 1). Only this kind of God can be called 'sovereign', or be trusted in times of suffering (Exod 4:11; Heb 12:3–13).

Open theists respond in turn that God's Lordship need not depend on his fixing all facts that will ever be. Indeed, William Hasker suggests that God's greatness is actually enhanced when he is understood to 'take risks' with the free choices he lovingly grants to his children, yet proves 'endlessly resourceful in achieving his ultimate purposes'.[2] Where traditionalists hold that biblical references to God 'repenting' and 'discovering' choices are anthropomorphic, openness advocates point out that anthropomorphism must stand for some more literal quality, and that it is difficult to see how these images could mean anything other than what they say about God.

Open theism is fiercely debated, and while it is hard to see it ever being reconciled with the classical view, it has at least prompted a serious biblical reassessment of long-standing assumptions about the attributes of God. Some have emerged from this process more convinced of the traditional view; others have undergone a radical 'conversion' to openness; and others have concluded that it is easier to see strains of both in Scripture than it is to systematise them. At the very least, each model holds that future is ultimately in God's hands rather than our own; that God will prevail redemptively in the cosmos; that fatalism is false, and that time and history are linear rather than cyclical. Beyond this, a good deal more debate would appear to lie ahead.

David Hilborn
Theological advisor to the Evangelical Alliance;
Chair, EA Commission on Unity and Truth among Evangelicals (ACUTE)

[1] Pinnock et al, *The Openness of God*, Downers Grove: Intervarsity press, 1994, p122.
[2] *The Openness of God*, p154.

PASSION

Two aspects of this debate are significant in the light of the 'Shepherd's Bush to King's Cross' journey. The first is that aspects of the Exodus story are often cited to support both sides of the debate. Yahweh enters into the sufferings of his people, goes to war against Pharaoh, negotiates with Moses and on two occasions seems to change his mind. An open God? And yet the whole narrative speaks of the certain promise of a known future. When Moses expresses doubt in God's call, he is told what the sign of God's presence with him will be – 'When you have brought the people out of Egypt, you will worship God on this mountain.' [Exod 3:12]

A future foreknown?

The second is that both sides are motivated by the same thing – a passion not to allow the glory of God to be diminished. The open theists believe that a God who cannot feel the pain of his creatures, who does not, in his love, take the 'risks' of openness is by definition cold, distant and unfeeling: and thereby 'less God' than he otherwise would be. Their detractors, on the other hand, believe that the Glory of God is diminished if he does not have the power in and of himself to see, know and shape the future.

Is this a case of a paradox that the Bible simply insists we accept?

 FELLOW TRAVELLERS

World Christians wanted

"Every Christian should be a World Christian, a global disciple, a Great Commission Christian, a servant of God," Robin Thomas writes. "But what does this mean? Three commitments ... characterise the World Christian (and should be the characteristic of every Christian). World Christians are:

> Committed to God's purpose for his world.
> Committed to God's people who are to carry out his purpose.
> Committed to working out God's purpose in daily life."

[Quoted in Stephen Gaukroger, *Why bother with mission?*, p14]

Burned up but not burnt out

Os Guinness recounts an incident from the life of one of the 'great men' of British history:
'Once, when Winston Churchill was on holiday staying with friends in the south of France, he came into the house on a chilly evening, sat down by the fireplace, and stared silently into the flames. Resin-filled pine logs were crackling, hissing, and spitting as they burned. Suddenly his familiar voice growled, "I know why logs spit. I know what it is to be consumed."'

Guiness contrasts this image with that of the burning bush, central to the call of Moses.

"But how was this great intimate of God called?" he asks. "He was arrested at the sight of a bush, burning yet not burned up – as if God were telling him from the very beginning that his call would set his life on fire, but the fire would not consume him."

[*The Call*, pp79, 80]

The Furnace of God's Love

Lord, I am poured out,
I come to you for renewal.
Lord, I am weary,
I come to you for refreshment.
Lord, I am worn,
I come to you for restoration.
Lord, I am lost,
I come to you for guidance.
Lord, I am troubled,
I come to you for peace.
Lord, I am lonely,
I come to you for love.
Come, Lord,
Come revive me
Come re-shape me
Come mould me in your image.
Re-cast me in the furnace of your love.
David Adam

[*Power Lines*, Triangle SPCK, 1992]

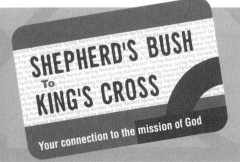

APPLICATIONS
A framework for mission and prayer

The four-fold description of God's passion given in Exodus 2:23–25 provides a valuable framework for our own consideration of both mission and prayer.

God Hears
The cry of the human heart

God Remembers
His people and his promise

God Sees
The very root of the human condition

God Knows
Every detail of our lives

Our prayers, our engagement in mission and our understanding of the why's and where's of God's plan can all be shaped and informed by these four activities.

- Try applying this framework to an area of concern in your life and mission.
- How might it change your approach to both mission and prayer if you knew beyond a doubt that, whatever area you are praying or working into, God has heard, remembered, seen and known?

To be seen is to be blessed

Ronald Rolheiser writes of the great importance of being 'seen'.

"A couple of years ago," he says, "a family that I know had a painful incident with their thirteen-year-old daughter. She was caught shoplifting ... she was stealing to get her father's attention. Her father, struggling in his relationship with her mother, did not give a lot of attention to his daughter. So she forced his hand. It was he that she demanded come to the police station to pick her up and settle things with the police. In doing

that he had to give his daughter his attention. He had to look at her."

Rolheiser says there is a deep longing inside us to be seen by those to whom we look up – our parents, our elders, our leaders, our teachers, our coaches, our pastors and our bosses. It is important to us, more than we generally imagine, that those who are above us look at us, recognise us, see us. ... To really see someone, especially someone who looks up to you, is to give that person a special blessing. The heart is set free by blessing from our elders.

[*Against an Infinite Horizon: The Finger of God in our Everyday Lives*, p21]

Street beggars often report that the most painful aspect of their predicament is not that people do not give them money – it is that so many people refuse even to make eye contact with them, preferring to run away rather than to see them. God does not treat the Hebrews with such indifference. He makes eye contact. He will rescue them, but first wants them to know that he has seen them.

- Who is there in your life by whom you feel the need to be 'seen'?
- Do you feel that God has 'seen you' in the sense that he saw the Hebrew slaves and all they were going through?
- Who is there in your life that would be blessed by knowing that you had 'seen' them?

Missio Dei applied

Gailyn Van Rheenen suggests, "At least five specific applications of the 'Mission of God' can be made:

- First, if mission flows from the character and nature of God, it cannot be neglected by the church. Mission, because it is God's, cannot be aborted.
- Second, since the mission is of God, God will equip people for the task.
- Third, the 'Mission of God' enables Christian missionaries to understand themselves under God's sovereignty. Christians should not under-

Sharing God's Passion
Henri Nouwen offers the following prophetic words: 'Mourn, my people, mourn. Let your pain rise up in your heart and burst forth in you with sobs and cries. Mourn for the silence that exists between you and your spouse. Mourn for the way you were robbed of your innocence. Mourn for the absence of a soft embrace, an intimate friendship, a life-giving sexuality...Cry loudly and deeply, and trust that your tears will make your eyes see that the Kingdom is close at hand, yes, at your fingertips!'

PASSION

take God's mission for self-glorification but for the glorification of God.

- Fourth, the 'Mission of God' implies sacrifice. It is a mission worth living for and dying for.
- Finally, this perspective enables the Christian communicator to recognise that because the mission is God's, it will succeed. Even though messengers fail and people reject the message, the mission of God continues."

[*Missions: Biblical Foundations and Contemporary Strategies*, p19]

- Do these five applications alter your view of mission? What difference does it make to your perspective to see mission as, first and foremost, the *missio Dei*?

Finding guidance

Finding the call of God is often a long and gruelling process – it was for Moses. Stephen Gaukroger in *Why Bother with Mission?* suggests that this is as true for the Christian 'greats' as for the rest of us:

'We often imagine that guidance comes easily to Christian workers. Don't they all have a hotline to heaven telling them where to work, when, and how to get there? Actually they are often as confused as we are! David Livingstone first thought God was calling him to China – and then went to Africa. William Carey felt he should serve God in Tahiti – and ended up in India.'
[*Why bother with mission?*, p132]

Do such stories encourage you to press on in your search for the call of God?

Jani Rubery, in *More Than A Job*, suggests five practical steps in seeking a true sense of vocation:
- Pray and fast to help you focus
- Listen to God
- Understand yourself – your gifts, passions, values, skills
- Talk to others for testing
- Open doors to explore options

[*More Than A Job*, p49]

Living with paradox

The suggestion that the 'Openness of God' debate can only be resolved by accepting a paradox raises the question of the many times in Scripture that we are asked to hold opposite extremes in tension. A useful phrase that captures this is VREONABA – 'Very rarely either-or, nearly always both-and'.

What are the circumstances in your life and faith in which God has called to accept a VREONABA solution?

CONNECTIONS
The Lord of the Rings by JRR Tolkein (Unwin Paperbacks)

Summary

Frodo Baggins lives in the Shire, in the northwestern lands of Middle-earth. Like all hobbits, he enjoys good food and a well-earned smoke. Following the sudden departure of his cousin Bilbo, Frodo becomes the possessor of a mysterious gold ring.

The wizard Gandalf explains the story of the ring: long ago, Sauron the Great made it on the fire-mountain. He was overthrown by the last great alliance of elves and men, one of whom subsequently lost the ring. Gandalf reveals to Frodo that this is the One Ring that could completely restore the power of the Dark Lord. It must, therefore, be returned to the only fire great enough to destroy it. As Ring-bearer, Frodo is called to deliver it into the Cracks of Doom on the fire-mountain, far away in Sauron's dark lands in the South.

Frodo is horrified to discover that he must deal with the Ring. Like many of us, he faces a task involving danger

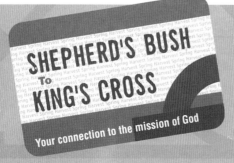
SHEPHERD'S BUSH TO KING'S CROSS
Your connection to the mission of God

and sacrifice, with no guarantee of success. How do these relate to Christian mission? Is it important to be motivated by passion? What does the Bible say about duty? How can we be encouraged to persevere with what we are called to?

Bible Study

1. 'Calling'

'I too once passed the Dimril Gate,' said Aragorn quietly; 'but though I also came out again, the memory is very evil. I do not wish to enter Moria a second time.'
'And I don't wish to enter it even once,' said Pippin.
'Nor me,' muttered Sam.
'Of course not!' said Gandalf. 'Who would? But the question is: who will follow me, if I lead you there?'
'I will,' said Gimli eagerly.
'I will,' said Aragorn heavily.
(Book II, A Journey in the Dark)

- **Read Exodus 3:4–15 and 4:1–17**. Why did Moses question God's call? How did God answer him?
- **Read Luke 4:14–30**. What was Jesus' mission? What difficulties did he encounter?
  Note: The widow and Naaman were not Israelites — redemption is not just for the Jews, which is what Jesus' hearers would have been expecting.

2. Duty — prepared to suffer

'But I count you blessed, Gimli son of Glóin: for your loss you suffer of your own free will, and you might have chosen otherwise. But you have not forsaken your companions, and the least reward that you shall have is that the memory of Lothlórien shall remain ever clear and unstained in your heart, and shall neither fade nor grow stale.' (Legolas, Book II, Farewell to Lórien)

- **Read Jeremiah 38:1–28**. How did Jeremiah fulfil his duty to God? What were the consequences?

Note: You may like to consider how this commission would have been hard for Jeremiah.
- **Read 2 Timothy 4:1–22**. How and why does Paul encourage us to persevere?

Implications

'So that was the job I felt I had to do when I started,' thought Sam; 'to help Mr Frodo to the last step and then die with him? Well, if that is the job then I must do it.' (Book VI, Mount Doom)

- Is God calling you to do something challenging? Are you ready for the cost?
- Is duty still a valid concept in our please-yourself culture?

From *Connect Bible Studies: What does the Bible say about... The Lord of the Rings*. ISBN 1 85999 634 5 published online by Damaris, and in print by Scripture Union – Linking the Word to the World. www.connectbiblestudies.com – these studies are available to buy from this site. ∎

THE BOOK STALL

Tony Lane, The Lion Concise History of Christian Thought, Lion
Tony Campolo, Let Me Tell You A Story, W Publishing Group, 2000
Gailyn Van Rheenen, Missions: Biblical Foundations and Contemporary Strategies, Zondervan, 1996
Terence E. Fretheim, Interpretation: Exodus
David Bosch, Transforming Mission: Paradigm Shifts in Theology of Mission, Orbis
Stephen Gaukroger, Why Bother with Mission?, IVP
Mark Stibbe, From Orphans to Heirs: Celebrating our Spiritual Adoption, Bible Reading Fellowship
Os Guinness, The Call, Carlisle: Spring Harvest / Paternoster, 2001
Jani Rubery, More Than A Job, Spring Harvest / Authentic, 2001
Tom and Christine Sine, Living on Purpose, Monarch
Phillip Greenslade & Selwyn Hughes, Cover to Cover God's Story, CWR

MERCY

1 DESTINATIONS AND DEFINITIONS
Mercy

mercy *noun* **(mercies) 1** kindness or forgiveness shown when punishment is possible or justified. **2** an act or circumstance in which these qualities are displayed, especially by God. **3** a tendency to be forgiving. **4** a piece of good luck; a welcome happening • *grateful for small mercies*. **5** compassion for the unfortunate. **at the mercy of someone** or **something** wholly in their or its power; liable to be harmed by them or it.
ETYMOLOGY: 12c: from French *merci*, from Latin *merces* reward.

© Copyright Chambers Harrap Publishers Ltd 2002

God chooses to show mercy to his people; carrying them, on eagles' wings, to freedom. Exodus is a story of mercy... ■

2 DISTRICT LINE
Mercy at Shepherd's Bush

"When Jimmy Carter became president of the United States of America, one of his first acts was to ask the Georgia Pardon and Parole Board if they would agree to release Mary Fitzpatrick into his custody so that she could take care of his daughter Amy. Mary Fitzpatrick was a poor black woman who, without the benefit of proper legal representation, had been convicted of murder and was serving a life sentence. She lived in the White House, 'performed her duties in an exemplary manner' and became very close to Amy. Later, she was granted a full pardon by the State of Georgia. It was an act of extraordinary grace on the Carters' part, not only to seek pardon for one who had been declared legally guilty of murder, but to invite her into their home and entrust their precious daughter into her care."
Derek Tidball
[*The Message of The Cross*, p193]

If the mission of God is rooted and grounded in his initiative and sustained by his passion, it is supremely expressed in his mercy. Throughout the Exodus narrative, the people of Israel are reminded that it is by God's free choice that they are saved. It is within his right and his power to punish – but he chooses to show mercy.

'Israel was a rabble of nomadic tribes, forged into a nation after the experience of redemption from slavery and genocide in ancient Egypt. The God who revealed himself to them as their liberator, and who entered into covenant with them, did so not because of any achievement or superiority on their part but because of God's unmerited and unconditioned love.'
Vinoth Ramachandra
[*Faiths in Conflict?*, p94]

This sense of a thread of mercy running through God's choices and actions is beautifully captured by the passage in Exodus 19:4 where God reminds Moses:

'"... 'You yourselves have seen what I did to Egypt, and how I carried you on eagles' wings and brought you to myself. Now if you obey me fully and keep my covenant, then out of all nations you will be my treasured possession. Although the whole earth is mine, you will be for me a kingdom of priests and a holy nation.' These are the words you are to speak to the Israelites."'

And in Exodus 33:19, when God chooses to reveal himself to Moses by the deepest and most intimate means, it is in mercy that he chooses to be known:

'And the LORD said, "I will cause all my goodness to pass in front of you, and I will proclaim my name, the LORD, in your presence. I will have mercy on whom I will have mercy, and I will have compassion on whom I will have compassion."'

Throughout the long and arduous journey from slavery to sonship, as God shows himself more and more fully to his people, mercy is, time and time again, his choice. ■

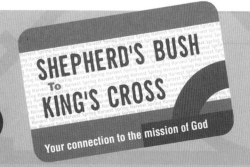

SHEPHERD'S BUSH
To
KING'S CROSS
Your connection to the mission of God

"The biblical use of eleos [Greek for mercy] portrays God as one who is deeply moved by human suffering and who has chosen to come to our aid despite the sin that makes us his enemies."
[*Applied Bible Dictionary*, Kingsway, 1990]

Close Up:

There is significant confusion in the contemporary church about the relationship between *grace* and *mercy*. Theologians have traditionally used a simple formula to distinguish the two ideas – **Grace** means **receiving** the blessing we don't deserve, while **Mercy** means **not receiving** the punishment we do. We often use the term *grace* to describe both, but it is an important pillar of Christian belief that mercy precedes grace. Before God can pour on us the blessing we haven't earned, he must first grant us amnesty for the punishment we have earned. Before he credits our current account, he acts to cancel our overdraft! Before he gives, he forgives. The generosity of God toward the Hebrew slaves contains both aspects of God's love. His relationship with the people of Israel does not only involve the giving of blessing – time and time again it involves the forgiving of sin.

If there is a danger in our contemporary culture it is that we will associate God's grace with an undefined, sentimental 'niceness'. The doctrine of mercy reminds us that God's generosity to us is more than this. It begins with the substantive removal of an actual barrier to love and life. We enter the courts of God as convicted felons – we leave with the words ringing in our ears 'the debt is cancelled – you are free to go'.

'Read Exodus. There was never a more rebellious generation, yet God gave his people chance after chance after chance. He is always offering a new start and the only sensible reaction is to take it.'
Alison Jacobs
[*The Road Through the Desert*, p51]

Main Lines

It is a common mistake, amongst Christians and non-Christians alike, to believe that the God of the Old Testament is the powerful, stern judge, burning with wrath and exacting punishment on a trembling creation, while the God of the New Testament shows mercy. This is not a view that can be supported by anything but a superficial reading of the Exodus story. God *is* revealed here in his sovereignty and power: there are spiritual and physical battles, plagues and signs, fire and clouds of smoke: but above all God is revealed in his mercy. Where power is present, it has the purpose of showing more of God's mercy.

The clear implication of the Exodus story is that mercy is not merely an *activity* of God but an *attribute*. In a sense God shows and offers mercy: but in a much deeper sense, he *is* mercy. When you get past the fear to the heart of God, mercy is what you find.

Three key aspects of this are revealed in the narrative, in which God is shown to be:

- The Sovereign who chooses
- The Father who adopts
- The Creator who gives life ■

MAIN LINE
Sovereign Selector: "I Am Who I Am"

Exodus 3:13–15

Moses said to God, "Suppose I go to the Israelites and say to them, 'The God of your fathers has sent me to you,' and they ask me, 'What is his name?' Then what shall I tell them?"
God said to Moses, "I AM WHO I AM. This is what you are to say to the Israelites: 'I AM has sent me to you.' "
God also said to Moses, "Say to the Israelites, 'The LORD, the God of your fathers – the God of Abraham, the God of Isaac and the God of Jacob – has sent me to you.' This is my name forever, the name by which I am to be remembered from generation to generation."

"The kyrie eleison of the ancient church has continued to be used in many liturgical forms of worship: 'Lord, have mercy upon us; Christ, have mercy upon us; Lord, have mercy upon us.'"
[*Evangelical Dictionary of Theology*, Marshall Pickering, 1984]

MERCY

God's revelation of himself as Yahweh lies at the very heart of the Exodus story. In one sense, the whole Exodus adventure is a commentary on these three verses – a sustained exploration of the name of God.

Exodus 3:14 is "one of the most puzzled over verses in the entire Hebrew Bible" (Terence Fretheim). It is also the foundation stone on which the unfolding story is built. D.S. Russell points out that "to the Hebrew mind the name is much more than simply a 'tag', an appellation. It contains within itself the 'soul', the character of the man, indicating what he is in the depths of his being." These verses are clearly intended to do more than reveal God's name: they are intended to reveal what he is like.

Whilst it is impossible in a few short words to explore the depths of this mysterious name – and millions have already been written in the attempt – it is possible to draw out from it key principles of the mission and mercy of God. The "I am" formula of the name of God tells us:

- That God is sovereign, and therefore free to choose. The miracle of mercy is that the all-powerful, all-knowing and all-seeing God chooses to bless.
- That God's actions will reveal his identity. The promise of mercy is that God will show us who he is by what he does.
- That God will prove his love: the power of mercy is that God's actions will be utterly consistent with his word. ■

✦ "I am who I am"

'Why is the revelation of God at Sinai so new that it smashes all categories and idols? What exactly is so brain hammering and conscience wracking? Is it the fire, the smoke, and the thunder? These are but pyrotechnics, the merest fringe sideshow, compared with the nuclear sunburst of the truth revealed – "I am who I am."'
Os Guinness
[The Call, p65]

The first key aspect of the "I am" of God is that it implies, within itself, an "I am not". The world of the

Old Testament was awash with gods – they had names and places, and 'covered' the different people groups and localities of the world. The Egyptians had their gods, and Moses' father-in-law Jethro was a priest to the gods of Midian. But their power was limited in time and space.

'Gods were thought by ancient Near Easterners to possess no power except on their own home ground. But not so here!'
[Expository Bible Commentary]

God's use of the mysterious formula "I am who I am" is a statement first and foremost of sovereignty. "I am not" the god of this mountain alone, whose power will fade as you walk away. "I am not" one god amongst many. "I am not" a god who can be named and tamed.

'This is a God who is on the move, who cannot be localized, who cannot be pinned down to one time and place.'
Terence Fretheim
[Interpretation: Exodus, p275]

God is not 'owned' by Israel in the way that each pagan tribe had their 'god'. He is the free, sovereign God of all the earth. He shows mercy because he may, not because he must. Israel will be set free not because their God is more powerful than Egypt's gods, but because the God – the all-powerful ruler of the universe – has chosen them as a means to show his mercy. ■

✦ "I will be what I will be"

The phrase translated "I am who I am" also carries the sense "I will be what I will be" – it points to the future and asserts that God's name and nature will be revealed in his actions.

'The answer given to Moses when he asks to know the "name" of the God who was sending him to Pharaoh is variously translated "I am what I am" or "I shall be what I shall be" or even "I shall be what I am". Perhaps the best way to understand this is that God declares

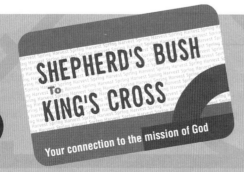

SHEPHERD'S BUSH to KING'S CROSS
Your connection to the mission of God

Close Up:

Linked to the idea of God's sovereignty is the reality of his anger or, more traditionally, wrath. Contemporary culture finds it difficult to talk about God as angry – and as a result has a diminished view of his mercy. The biblical view of God's anger tells us:

- God's anger is a considered response to the fallenness of the creation and the sin of his people. It is not an uncontrolled emotional outburst.

  'The anger of God is nevertheless no emotional outburst, because of his prior decree, forewarning, pleadings, judgments, and endless endurance with the wilful disobedience of his own people. After all, he had helped them many times in their distresses, but without any apparent change in Israel's spiritual condition.'

  [*Expository Bible Commentary*]

- God's anger is not an alternative to his love, but a sign of it. When God's good plans for his creation and for his people are spoiled, his anger is a measure of his care. If God were to turn a blind eye to sin, it could only be on the basis either that he doesn't know the difference between good and evil or that he knows the difference and doesn't care. God's wrath is an expression of the fact that he does know the difference – and does care.

  'Orge [cf Hebrews 3:11] is the usual word for the "wrath" of God and points to the strong and settled opposition of God's holy nature to all that is evil. God is not passive in the face of wrongdoing; he actively opposes it. "Wrath" may not be the perfect word with which to express this (as used of men it implies lack of self-control and the like that do not apply to God). But it seems the best word we have and it does bring out God's passionate opposition to evil and his concern for the right. Those who reject its use are in danger of misrepresenting God as one who does not care.'

  [*Expository Bible Commentary*]

Without the wrath of God, there is no mercy of God. If God had no choice but to show mercy, then the mercy shown would have no meaning. God's mercy is real because he chooses to forgive when the legitimate and expected thing would be to maintain his anger and act on it. If I received a letter telling me that a debt of £10,000 had been cancelled, I would leap for joy – but only if I really did owe the £10,000. If there were no debt in the first place, there would be no power in its cancellation. The wrath of God reminds us that the debt is real, and that its cancellation – God's mercy – is therefore also real.

that he will be known personally only through his future actions. Israel will come to know the personal "name" of God (which sums up his eternal character) through his redemptive actions in history.'

Vinoth Ramachandra

[*Faiths in Conflict?*, p187]

"The Jewish people in the ancient world were very different from the Greeks," Tony Campolo writes.

'If you had asked the Greeks what they thought about God, they would have talked about God's essence. They would have said such things as, 'God is the ground of all being!' or, 'God is the unmoved mover!' They might have used words like 'omnipotence', 'omniscience' and 'omnipresence', in order to describe what God is.

'The Hebrew people, on the other hand, did not even try to get at the essence of God. They knew it was past finding out. Instead of talking about what God is, the

MERCY

Jews always talked about what God did. If you had asked them about God, they would have said, 'Our God is the One who delivered us from the hands of the Egyptians and brought us into the Promised Land. Our God is the One who defended us against the enemies, has guided us, and has made us the chosen people.' The Jews would have talked about what God has done and is doing and would have contended that all we can know about God is what we can deduce from His actions. They knew that they were in a covenant relationship with God, and that God would not break that covenant. They knew that God would go on loving them, no matter what – because of what He had done.'

[*Let me tell you a story*, Tony Campolo]

Here the sovereign God asserts that the mercy he shows to Israel is the means by which he has chosen to make himself known. ■

✦ "I shall be what I am"

Not only will God show who he is by what he does, but his actions will prove beyond doubt his commitment to his chosen people. When the Hebrews see, by what God does, what he is like, then they will see that he is mercy.

'This title [I AM WHO I AM] defines God to be the ever-present deity who is consistently faithful to his promises.'
Gailyn Van Rheenen
[*Missions: Biblical Foundations and Contemporary Strategies*, p16]

"The very name of the God of Israel," Stephen Travis writes, "means that he will be for ever what he now is: he is committed to his people for ever."
[*The Bible as a whole*, p46]

The conflict with Pharaoh becomes an outworking of this promise. The Hebrew slaves have been subjected to the cruel sovereignty of Pharaoh, the all-powerful presence in their lives. But God will show them a different kind of power. He is the all-powerful sovereign, yet he will rule them with mercy and love. Terence Fretheim contrasts Exodus 3:7-10 (God's promise of mercy) with Exodus 5: 5-18 (the cruel actions of a powerful dictator):

'Who will finally be recognized as the sovereign one, Yahweh or Pharaoh? Whom will Israel serve? But an oft-forgotten parallel issue is: What kind of sovereignty is being exercised? Pharaoh's and Yahweh's ways of being sovereign are contrasted in the narrative.'
[*Interpretation: Exodus*, p17]

"In Egypt, the Israelites were driven by whips," Mark Stibbe says. "In the Exodus, they were drawn by cords of love."
[*From Orphans to Heirs*, p37]

In Brief:
God's revelation of his name to Moses, far from portraying an Old Testament God in contrast to the God of the New, points towards the merciful God ultimately revealed in Jesus.

The miracle of mercy experienced by Moses and the Hebrew slaves is the miracle offered universally in Christ, when the "I am" of Shepherd's Bush finds full expression in the King's Cross.

'The outcasts whom Jesus befriended and to whom he gave a new identity as members of his disciple-community were caught out completely unawares by the shattering generosity of God's acceptance, experienced through Jesus.'
Vinoth Ramachandra
[*Faiths in Conflict?*, p102]

This is the God, consistent always to his name and nature, celebrated by the Apostle Paul in Ephesians 2:4 as 'rich in mercy'.

'Just as we might say that a Texas tycoon is "rich in oil", so Paul writes it as a matter of fact that God is "rich in mercy". The pagan world was full of fear, and the Christian gospel set out to replace that fear of the gods or the fates, or even life itself, with love for and trust in God. "Rich in mercy" was good news to the ancient world and it is good news today.'
J.B. Phillips ■

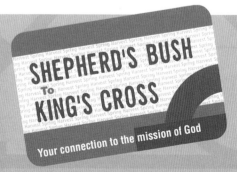

MAIN LINE
Perfect Parent: "Israel is my son"

'The supreme revelation about God in the Scriptures is that he is the eternal Father. In a sense, this is God's highest name. ... The father-child relationship to which God calls us corresponds to the way we have been created, that is, in God's image. It is the fulfilment of our relationship with God.'
Chawkat Moucarry

Not only does Exodus speak of the sovereign God who chooses to show mercy – it also shows God as father, and introduces the important concept of adoption. In Exodus 4:22–23, when Moses has accepted the call of God and is preparing to return Egypt to confront Pharaoh, God reminds him of his task with these words:
Then say to Pharaoh, 'This is what the LORD says: Israel is my firstborn son, and I told you, "Let my son go, so he may worship me."'

"God chose Israel out of all the nations of the world to be his adopted son," Mark Stibbe writes. "He chose one of the most insignificant groups of people and, in the process, made them the most significant nations in history. He took a very ordinary community of people and conferred on them the most extraordinary purpose. Why? Because our God is an adopting father. Out of sheer grace he chooses to embrace people in the enfolding circle of his love."

[*From Orphans to Heirs*, p35]

When the prophet Hosea looks back to the Exodus to celebrate the works of God, it is in these terms that he speaks:
*"When Israel was a child, I loved him,
	and out of Egypt I called my son...
I led them with cords of human kindness,
	with ties of love;
I lifted the yoke from their neck
	and bent down to feed them."*
[Hosea 11:1,4]

From this point on, adoption becomes one of the key threads of Scripture, a central pillar in the ministry of Jesus, captured in the Lord's Prayer. No other image reveals the mercy of God more fully and movingly than the idea that he is our perfect parent, not only choosing and saving us, but adopting us into the inner circle of his family. ■

Close Up:
R. Hammerton-Kelly asserts that adoption is a key principle in the Exodus narrative, introduced as the only image adequate to explain the relationship Yahweh offers to his people:

'In order to express this new and characteristically Mosaic theology, the Yahwists chose the image of adoption. The relationship between God and his people is that of father and adopted son'
[*God the Father: Theology and Patriarchy in the Teaching of Jesus* (Fortress Press, 1979), p31]

MAIN LINE
Caring Creator: "proclaimed in all the earth"

In Exodus 9:16 the confrontation between Yahweh and the gods of Egypt is in full force. God sends Moses to Pharaoh with a message of warning and rebuke, in which the Egyptian dictator is told:

"I have raised you up for this very purpose, that I might show you my power and that my name might be proclaimed in all the earth."

The fight for the freedom of the slaves is not an end in itself, but has a higher purpose – that the Glory of God should be revealed to the very ends of the earth. The battle is not for the sake of Israel alone, but for the whole creation.

"Returning hate for hate multiplies hate, adding deeper darkness to a night already devoid of stars. Darkness cannot drive out darkness; only light can do that. Hate cannot drive out hate; only love can do that. ... Forgiveness does not mean ignoring what has been done or putting a false label on an evil act. It means, rather, that the evil act no longer remains a barrier to the relationship."
Martin Luther King Jr

MERCY

'Israel had been entrusted with a unique historical experience of Yahweh's character and purpose for his creation. It is this that enables them to bear witness to his uniqueness as the living God (e.g. Is 43:8–13). Israel existed as a nation at all only because of Yahweh's intention to redeem people from every nation. While Yahweh works in all nations, in no nation other than Israel did he act for the sake of all nations.'

Vinoth Ramachandra

[Faiths in Conflict?, p96]

Terence Fretheim asserts that the language of the Exodus narrative clearly indicates that it is the Creator God who has spoken to Moses, and that the whole book is "shaped in a decisive way by a creation theology. ... It is the Creator God who redeems Israel from Egypt. God's work in creation has been shown to be life-giving, life-preserving, and life-blessing (e.g. 1:7, 12, 20). What God does in redemption is in the service of these endangered divine goals in and for the creation. ... Not only is an *experience* of God's work as Creator necessary for participation in the exodus – otherwise there would be no people to redeem, an *understanding* of God's work as Creator is indispensable for the proper interpretation of what happens – there would be no exodus *as we know it* without its having been informed by that understanding... A creation theology provides the *cosmic purpose* behind God's redemptive activity on Israel's behalf. While the liberation of Israel is the focus of God's activity, it is not the ultimate purpose. The deliverance of Israel is ultimately for the sake of all creation (see 9:16). The issue for God is finally not that God's name be made known in Israel but that it be declared to the entire earth. God's purpose in these events is creation-wide. What is at stake is God's mission for the world."

[Interpretation: Exodus, p13]

Close Up:

James D Newsome cites two key examples of 'creation language' in Exodus: in Exodus 2:3, Moses is hidden in a papyrus basket among the reeds of the Nile. "The Hebrew word behind 'basket' is used only in this story and in one other – the story of Noah, where the same Hebrew word refers to the ark (Genesis 6–8)."

[Exodus – Interpretation Bible Studies, p9]

In Exodus 14:21 a 'strong east wind' blows all night to push back the waters of the Red Sea. The text "uses the same Hebrew noun (*ruach*) as that in Genesis 1:2: 'and the Spirit [*ruach*] of God was moving over the face of the waters' ... The text of Exodus 14 intends the readers to understand that Yahweh, the God of Israel, is the creator of the heaven and earth, and that all other gods are no gods at all."

[Exodus – Interpretation Bible Studies, p54]

When Moses and the people celebrate God's victory in The Song of Moses in Exodus 15:1-18, in which the divine name appears ten times, the language is thoroughly creational, presenting the events as a new creation.

'The appearance of creation motifs in the song suggests that Yahweh's redemption of Israel with a high hand and an outstretched arm is a renewal of the creation mandate. The divine saving purposes for the world are in some way bound up with Yahweh's victory over Egypt at the sea.'

Andreas J. Köstenberger & Peter T. O'Brien

[Salvation to the Ends of the Earth, p32]

In Brief:

The God who meets with Moses and liberates the Hebrew slaves is the Creator God, ruler of the universe. His choice of Israel and his victory over Pharaoh both indicate the promise and possibility of mercy for the whole earth. Not only has the God of Abraham not forgotten his people – neither has the God of Adam forgotten his world.

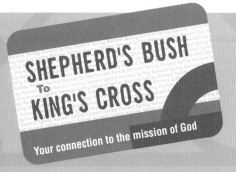

SHEPHERD'S BUSH
To
KING'S CROSS
Your connection to the mission of God

"Both Israel and humankind will ultimately be judged not only by God's justice, but also by God's mercy. Indeed, Exodus makes clear that when divine judgement and divine mercy collide, divine mercy will prevail."

James D. Newsome

Close Up:

"The 'many other people' who left Egypt with the Hebrews [Exodus 12:38] were composed of Egyptians (some 'feared the word of the LORD' in 9:20), perhaps some of the old Semitic population left from the Hyksos era and slaves native to other countries. Some of this group must be part of the 'rabble' (ha'sapsup lit., 'a collection') mentioned later in Numbers 11:4. Thus the promise to Abraham in Genesis 12:3, of a blessing to 'all peoples on the earth', received another fulfilment in this swarm of foreigners who were impressed enough by the power of God to leave Egypt with Israel after all the plagues had been performed. Another aspect of God's display of his power was so that the Egyptians could, if they only would, be evangelized (7:5; 8:10, 19; 9:14, 16, 29-30; 14:4, 18)."

[Expository Bible Commentary]

"The election of Israel is assuredly one of the most fundamental pillars of the biblical worldview, and of Israel's historical sense of identity," Christopher Wright writes. "It is vital to insist that although the belief in their election could be (and was) distorted into a narrow doctrine of national superiority, that move was resisted in Israel's own literature (e.g. Deut 7:7ff.). The affirmation is that the Yahweh, the God who had chosen Israel, was also the creator, owner and Lord of the whole world (Deut 10:14f), and that Yahweh had chosen Israel in relation to his purpose for the world, not just for Israel. The election of Israel was not tantamount to a rejection of the nations, but explicitly for their ultimate benefit. Thus, rather than asking if Israel itself 'had a mission', in the sense of being 'sent' anywhere, we need to see the missional nature of Israel's existence in relation to the mission of God in the world. Israel's mission was to be something, not to go somewhere."

[*Christian Mission and the Old Testament: Matrix or Mismatch?*,
www.martynmission.cam.ac.uk]

BRANCH LINE
The currency of mercy is forgiveness

Tony Campolo tells of a remarkable conversation between two world-known presidents that illustrates the power of forgiveness:

'President Clinton tells of his first meeting with Nelson Mandela. In his conversation with this great leader of South Africa, the president said, "When you were released from prison, Mr Mandela, I woke my daughter at three o'clock in the morning. I wanted her to see this historic event. As you marched from the cellblock across the yard to the gate of the prison, the camera focused in on your face. I have never seen such anger, and even hatred, in any man as was expressed on your face at that time. That's not the Nelson Mandela I know today. What was all that about?"

'Mandela answered, "I'm surprised that you saw that, and I regret that the cameras caught my anger. As I walked across the courtyard that day I thought to myself; They've taken everything from you that matters. Your cause is dead. Your family is gone. Your friends have been killed. Now they're releasing you, but there's nothing left for you out there. And I hated them for what they had taken from me. Then, I sensed an inner voice saying to me, "Nelson! For twenty-seven years you were their prisoner, but you were always a free man! Don't allow them to make you into a free man, only to turn you into their prisoner!" An unforgiving spirit creates bitterness in our soul and imprisons our spirits. A failure to forgive imprisons us.'

[*Let Me Tell You A Story*]

Throughout biblical and Christian history, there has been an understanding that mercy is expressed in forgiveness – the 'lost art of forgiving' is mercy with its boots on: mercy that refuses to remain a theory and insists on getting involved in real lives. Just as the mercy of God brought freedom for the Hebrew salves, so the practice of mercy and forgiveness is a source of freedom in our world.

"When I bow before his love he is not slow to come; rather he has already come, for he loves me so much more than I, poor creature, can ever love him. And love shows itself in action, as for the Prodigal Son. Rising up is a fact, leaving the pigs is a fact. The soul must say with sincerity, 'Now I will arise and go to my Father.'"
Carlo Carretto

MERCY

'After the 1939–1945 war, Corrie ten Boom cared for those who had suffered at the hands of the Nazis. She found that survivors who chose to forgive those who had harmed them were able to move on and rebuild their lives, regardless of the remaining physical scars; those who did not remained bitter and continued as invalids. The choice to forgive, painful though it may be, can bring a freedom that speeds the journey to wholeness.'
Pamela Evans

[*Building the Body: Transforming Relationships in the Local Church,* p37]

Chris Carrier, who was abducted, attacked and shot as a ten-year-old in Florida, leaving him with permanent disabilities and disfigurement, and who chose to forgive the man who attacked him, writes: "Forgiveness is a gift – it is mercy. It is a gift I that I have received and also given away. In both cases, it has been completely satisfying."

Those who have received mercy are called to become, in their turn, bearers of mercy. "It is our birthright, as the followers of Jesus," Tom Wright says, "to breathe in true divine forgiveness day by day, as the cool, clear air which our spirituals lungs need instead of the grimy, germ-laden air that is pumped at us from all sides. And, once we start inhaling God's fresh air, there is a good chance that they will start to breathe it out, too. As we learn what it is like to be forgiven, we begin to discover that it is possible, and indeed joyful, to forgive others."

[*The Lord and His Prayer*]

✦ Calling as an encounter with the mercy of God

The underlying presence of the mercy of God in the Exodus story draws attention to the place of mercy in calling and mission. Just as the people of Israel find their identity and mission in God's mercy for them, so Moses himself has been preserved through God's mercy, and this is foundational to his calling. Before we can go and give in response to the mission of God, we must first draw near and receive.

"In other words," Os Guinness writes, "there is more to God's call than simply sending us out – the commissioning, as calling is usually thought to be. Certainly, it ends by 'sending us out', but it begins by 'singling us out' – we are called by name – and it continues by 'standing us up'. As we respond to the call of our Creator, we rise to our feet, not only physically but also in every sense of the word, to be the people he alone knows we are capable of being. Like a coach bringing out the full capacity of each member of the team, or a conductor bringing out the deepest potential of the orchestra, God's call resonates in us at depths no other call can reach and draws us on and out and up to heights no other call can scale or see."

[*The Call*, p84]

Before we can 'throw ourselves into' the action and activity of mission, we must first throw ourselves onto God's mercy. No other foundation will serve as the basis for Christian mission. Charles de Foucauld, founder of the Little Brothers of Jesus, expressed this life-decision in his Prayer of Abandonment:

*My Father,
I abandon myself to you,
do with me as you will.*

*Whatever you may do with me
I thank you.
I am prepared for anything,
I accept everything,
provided your will is fulfilled in me
and in all creatures.
I ask for nothing more my God.*

*I place my soul in your hands.
I give it to you, my God,
with all the love of my heart
because I love you.*

*And for me it is a necessity of love,
this gift of myself,
this placing of myself in your hands without reserve,
in boundless confidence,
because you are my Father.*

SHEPHERD'S BUSH to KING'S CROSS
Your connection to the mission of God

FELLOW TRAVELLERS
Responding to the name of God

Your Name is Love…
Lord, Your Name is Love,
do not reject me, lost and astray.
Your Name is Power –
strengthen me, feeble and falling.
Your name is Light,
flood my suffering soul.
Your Name is Peace,
calm my troubled heart.
Your Name is Mercy –
never cease from showing mercy to me and mine.
Father John of Kronstadt

[trans. Jenny Robertson, *Windows to Eternity*, p148]

Mercy versus fear

Do you know what the most frequent command in the Bible turns out to be? What instruction, what order, is given, again and again, by God, by angels, by Jesus, by prophets and apostles? What do you think – 'Be good'? 'Be holy, for I am holy'? Or, negatively, 'Don't sin'? 'Don't be immoral'? No. The most frequent command in the Bible is: 'Don't be afraid. Don't be afraid. Fear not. Don't be afraid.'
N.T. Wright

[*Following Jesus: Biblical Reflections on Discipleship*, p56]

APPLICATIONS
Merciful God – merciful people

John Piper finds the connection between the mercy and mission of God in the story of Jonah:

'Jonah tried to run away because he knew God would be gracious to the people and forgive them. The point of the book is not the fish. It's about mission and racism and ethnocentrism. The point is this: be merciful like God, not miserly like Jonah. For Jonah, "be merciful" meant to be a missionary.'
[*Let the Nations Be Glad: The Supremacy of God in Missions*, p188]

- How might a deeper sense of God's mercy change your view of mission?
- Are there people you struggle to forgive to whom God might long to show mercy?
- What new and different activities might you engage in if your definition of mission was *'God using me to show his mercy'*?

Following the "I am not" God

Timothy Yates, in *Mission – An Invitation To God's Future* explores the creation-wide nature of the mission of God:

'Christianity cannot be a family religion, a tribal religion, or the religion of a particular people or nation. It cannot be a male religion. And it cannot be the political religion of a particular government or rule. If these religious forms develop, Christianity becomes so deformed as to be unrecognisable.'

- Are you aware of examples of mission being distorted because it has been made too local and tribal, and 'owned' by its missionaries?
- What might a bigger picture of who God is do to your personal sense of calling and mission?

THE BOOK STALL

Johann Christoph Arnold, The Lost Art of Forgiving, Plough: available as a free e-book *Why Forgive?* from www.bruderhof.com
Stephen Dray, Exodus, Free to Serve, Crossway
James D. Newsome, Interpretation Bible Studies – Exodus
Tim Jeffrey and Steve Chalke, Connect!, Spring Harvest / Authentic, 2003
Samuel Escobar, A Time for Mission: The Challenge for Global Christianity, IVP, 2003
Vinoth Ramachandra and Howard Peskett, The Message of Mission, IVP, 2003
James Beilby and Paul Eddy, Ed., Divine Foreknowledge: Four Views, Paternoster, 2001
Gregory Ganssle, Ed., God and Time: Four Views, Paternoster, 2001

Part Two:
GOD DELIVERS
SALVATION & FREEDOM

Bible Reading, Jonah 2:1-10

[1]From inside the fish Jonah prayed to the LORD his God. [2]He said:

"In my distress I called to the LORD, and he answered me.
From the depths of the grave I called for help,
and you listened to my cry.
[3]You hurled me into the deep, into the very heart of the seas, and the currents swirled about me;
all your waves and breakers swept over me.
[4]I said, 'I have been banished from your sight;
yet I will look again toward your holy temple.'
[5]The engulfing waters threatened me, the deep surrounded me;
seaweed was wrapped around my head.
[6]To the roots of the mountains I sank down;
the earth beneath barred me in forever.
But you brought my life up from the pit, O LORD my God.

[7]"When my life was ebbing away, I remembered you, LORD,
and my prayer rose to you, to your holy temple.

[8]"Those who cling to worthless idols forfeit the grace that could be theirs.
[9]But I, with a song of thanksgiving, will sacrifice to you.
What I have vowed I will make good. Salvation comes from the LORD."

[10]And the LORD commanded the fish, and it vomited Jonah onto dry land.

Overview

Jonah comes to his senses and prays the most honest prayer of his life, promising to obey and get on with what God is asking him to do.

He learns a tough, yet important lesson – you can't swim in the ocean of grace if you paddle in the puddles of sin (v 8). His prayer ends with a declaration of faith; 'Salvation comes from the Lord!' (v 9)

God delivers Jonah. And he makes the most inauspicious entry of any servant of the Lord. Covered in fish vomit, he is dumped on a beach.

Many read this story and spot the great fish yet fail to see the great God!

He is the Lord who delivers.

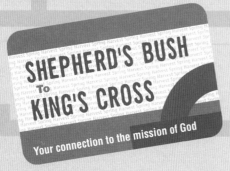

SHEPHERD'S BUSH
To
KING'S CROSS
Your connection to the mission of God

NOTES

SALVATION

NOTES

Exodus 3:16–20

¹⁶"Go, assemble the elders of Israel and say to them, 'The LORD, the God of your fathers – the God of Abraham, Isaac and Jacob – appeared to me and said: 'I have watched over you and have seen what has been done to you in Egypt. ¹⁷And I have promised to bring you up out of your misery in Egypt into the land of the Canaanites, Hittites, Amorites, Perizzites, Hivites and Jebusites – a land flowing with milk and honey.'
¹⁸"The elders of Israel will listen to you. Then you and the elders are to go to the king of Egypt and say to him, 'The LORD, the God of the Hebrews, has met with us. Let us take a three-day journey into the desert to offer sacrifices to the LORD our God.' ¹⁹But I know that the king of Egypt will not let you go unless a mighty hand compels him. ²⁰So I will stretch out my hand and strike the Egyptians with all the wonders that I will perform among them. After that, he will let you go."

Introduction

When I lived for a time in Paris, I met a talented young actor named Damien. An agnostic Catholic, he was wrestling with many deep questions of his own identity and purpose. At the prestigious École Jacques Lecoq theatre school, he was taught that there is no acting, only being. Before you can act a part, you must know the centre of your character so deeply that you effectively become them. Asked by a Christian friend to help out with an Easter sketch at a Paris church, Damien was given the part of the penitent thief. This was the man who, knowing that he deserved the punishment inflicted on him, nonetheless decided with his dying breath to seek salvation. Why did he do that? 'I cannot play this part,' Damien told himself, 'until I know.' Why did he let go of his self-sufficiency and reach out for help?

And then it came to him. In a Saturday afternoon rehearsal, hanging as if crucified, reaching for the centre of this character, Damien understood. This man reached out to Jesus because he couldn't, for himself, resolve his life. The guilt that he carried; the unanswered questions; the burden of anxiety and fear; his anger; his pain: for any of these to be resolved before death, he needed someone outside of himself to speak healing. He could

not declare himself forgiven – but he could receive forgiveness offered to him. Damien understood in that moment that this was what he, too, needed. He began a journey with God later that day that brought colossal changes in his life. Self was not enough. He needed God. He needed salvation.

This contemporary story captures the heart of the deliverance that is evidenced in the Exodus narrative and continues throughout the biblical record. Salvation and liberation are not things we can win for ourselves – we can't buy them, earn them, manufacture them or make them happen. We can't work them or worry them into being. We can only receive them. Salvation is not what we do to find God: it is what God does to find us. And it is pictured, as powerfully as in any story ever told, in God's liberation of the Hebrew slaves.

The passion of God for his people is not left in the realms of propositional truth alone: it is expressed in action. God takes action to bring his people out of their misery. Salvation and freedom are his and his alone to deliver – and he does. ∎

SALVATION

DESTINATIONS AND DEFINITIONS
Salvation

salvation *noun* **1** the act of saving someone or something from harm. **2** a person or thing that saves another from harm. **3** *relig* the liberation or saving of man from the influence of sin, and its consequences for his soul.
ETYMOLOGY: 13c: from Latin *salvatus* saved, from *salvare* to save.

save *verb (saved, saving)* **1** to rescue, protect or preserve someone or something from danger, evil, loss or failure. **2** to use economically so as to prevent or avoid waste or loss. **3** *intrans* to be economical, especially with money • *We're saving for the future.* **4** to reserve or store for later use. **5** to spare from potential unpleasantness or inconvenience • *Doing a dissertation saves you having to do two exams* • *That will save you having to make another trip.* **6** to obviate or prevent. **7** *sport* to prevent (a ball or shot) from reaching the goal; to prevent (a goal) from being scored by the opposing team. **8** *tr & intr, relig* to deliver from the influence or consequences of sin; to act as a saviour • *Jesus saves.* **9** *computing* to transfer (data, the contents of a computer file, etc) onto a disk or tape for storage. *noun* **1** an act of saving a ball or shot, or of preventing a goal • *He made a great save in that match.* **2** *computing* the saving of data onto a disk or tape. *prep* (*sometimes* **save for**) except • *Save for one, John lost all the books* • *We found all the tickets save one.* *conj*, old use (*often* **save that**) were it not that; unless • *I would have gone with her, save that she had already left.* **savable** *adj.* **saver** *noun.* **saved by the bell** *often exclamation* rescued or saved from a difficult or unpleasant situation by a welcome interruption.
ETYMOLOGY: from the bell which indicates the end of a round in a boxing match. **save one's** or **someone's bacon** to enable oneself or them to escape or come off unscathed from a difficult situation. **save one's** or **someone's face** to prevent oneself or them from appearing foolish or wrong; to avoid humiliation. **save one's** or **someone's skin** or **neck** to save one's or their life • *You really saved my skin when you snared the tiger.* **save** or **keep something for a rainy day** see

under rainy. **save the day** to prevent something from disaster, failure, etc • *Colin saved the day by remembering to bring the map of the maze with him.*
ETYMOLOGY: 13c: from French *sauver*, from Latin *salvare*, from *salvus* safe.

© *Copyright Chambers Harrap Publishers Ltd 2002*

God takes action for the rescue of his people: it is by his initiative alone that they are saved. Exodus is a story of salvation... ∎

DISTRICT LINES
Seeing salvation

The unfolding narrative of God's confrontation with Pharaoh, of the warnings and plagues, of the Passover lamb and the crossing of the sea demonstrates:

- **The nature of salvation:** God can and will act for the liberation of his people
- **The scope of salvation:** liberation is at one and the same time individual, corporate and universal.

And it points towards:

- **The fulfilment of salvation:** God's ultimate rescue plan in the liberating work of Jesus.

Nature of salvation

'God is not looking for people who will work for him, so much as he is looking for people who will let him work for them.'
John Piper

'The Exodus is the supreme model of Yahweh's redemptive action"
Chris Wright
[*Christian Mission and the Old Testament: Matrix or Mismatch?*]

At the heart of the Exodus narrative – in the promises given to Moses by God and in the events by which they are fulfilled – there is a consistent underlying thread:

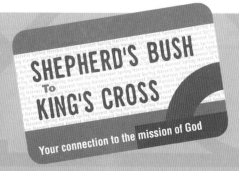

SHEPHERD'S BUSH TO KING'S CROSS
Your connection to the mission of God

"Christianity is the only major religion to have as its central event the suffering and degradation of its God."
Bamber Gascoigne,
The Christians

Close Up:

'Walter Brueggemann points out what an astonishing variety of "verbs of deliverance" Exodus uses of God. He "brings out", "rescues", "delivers", "saves" and "redeems" his people. Each verb has its own nuance. In Hebrew, they come from different spheres of life and evoke images of a geographical exit, of being pulled out of danger, of transforming a situation, of decisive military action and of being released from slavery. But the remarkable thing is that God "is the subject of all these verbs". The exodus was his initiative, and he carried it through successfully to completion. The covenant God of Israel and sovereign Lord of creation acted in faithfulness, compassion, justice and power to grant his people liberty.'
Derek Tidball

deliverance is not something the Hebrews can do for themselves, even with God's help: it is something Yahweh will do for them. At the height of the drama, when the slaves have taken their night-time flight from Pharaoh and are being pursued by his heavily-armed troops, they stand in fear and trembling; trapped between the desert and the sea. Moses says to the people:

'Do not be afraid. Stand firm and you will see the deliverance the LORD will bring you today. The Egyptians you see today you will never see again. The LORD will fight for you; you need only to be still.'
[Exodus 14:13]

Moses' words both set the stage for the central drama of deliverance – the crossing of the Red Sea – and reveal the core reality of salvation: that it is not about what we do but about what God does for us.

It is a central pillar of the story that God did for the slaves what they could not do for themselves. He did not simply help them to find freedom, nor so transform and equip them that they were able to break free: he himself became the key player in the drama. ∎

In Brief:

No amount of training, cajoling, persuading or empowering could have enabled the slaves to create their own deliverance: God and God alone could make the difference. It is by this token that the Exodus remains a central paradigm or model of salvation for the Christian church.

Scope of salvation

'There is not one square inch of the entire creation about which Jesus Christ does not cry out "this is mine – this belongs to me."'
Abraham Kuyper

On the surface, the deliverance of Israel is about an end to their slavery. But it is clear from the text that much more is happening. God's acts of deliverance will affect the newly freed slaves in every dimension of their lives.

And it is not the slaves alone who will be changed. God's acts are presented as cosmic in their implications – relating not only to Israel and Egypt but to the whole creation. Because the God who acts for Israel's salvation is the Creator God, working out his plans for the whole cosmos, the salvation he offers is, by definition, cosmic in scope. ∎

"As Albert Schweitzer once put it, Jesus was called to throw himself on the wheel of world history, so that, even though it crushed him, it might start to turn in the opposite direction."
Tom Wright

SALVATION

Close Up:

The universal scope of salvation was often misunderstood by the Hebrews themselves, and is often hidden in the Old Testament record: but it is present all the same. As Chris Wright has noted, "The historic promise that God would bless the nations through Israel developed into an eschatological vision that is found particularly in Israel's worship (cf. the universal scope of Psa 47, 87, 96) and in some of the prophets (Amos 9:12, Isa 19:23–25, 49:6, 56:1–8, 60:1-3, 66:19–21, Zech 2:1 etc). These texts are quite breathtaking in their universal scope. Ultimately there would be those of the nations who would not merely be joined to Israel, but would come to be identified as Israel, with the same names, privileges and responsibilities before God."

[*Christian Mission and the Old Testament: Matrix or Mismatch?*]

In Brief:

'God has still got his sights firmly fixed on all the nations, even at the precise moment when he chooses one nation to serve him in the world!'
Phillip Greenslade & Selwyn Hughes
[*Cover to Cover God's Story*, p137]

Fulfilment of salvation

If the Exodus is viewed only in its direct, Old Testament, setting it could be said to offer the *promise* of salvation for the whole earth, but not its fulfilment. Viewed, though, in the wider biblical context, the Exodus offers more than that:

The Exodus not only shows *in itself* God's salvation, it also points beyond itself to a time when God's promise-plan will "marvellously and mysteriously" come to fruition in "his Servant-King who, by his blood poured out as a sacrificial offering, inaugurates the new covenant

agreement, initiates a new Exodus from sin and death, and guarantees the coming of God's kingdom!"
Phillip Greenslade & Selwyn Hughes
[*Cover to Cover God's Story*, p221]

The New Testament consistently asserts that God's saving actions in the Exodus story serve as pictures or models of all that is achieved in Christ.

"What is being claimed here is astonishing," Derek Tidball writes. "It is saying that all that happened through the Passover lamb in Israel's experience happens now through Jesus in our experience. His sacrifice on the cross brings sinners to judgment, principalities and powers to destruction, those under sentence of death to redemption, the oppressed into freedom and its participants into membership of a consecrated people."
[*The Message of The Cross*, p65] ■

MAIN LINE
Salvation at King's Cross

'Christ... is to us just what his cross is. You do not understand Christ till you understand his cross.'
P T Forsyth

The Exodus is not only a story of all that God did to save Israel; it is also a paradigm of all that God does in salvation. The promise is made at the Shepherd's Bush: but it finds its fulfilment in the King's Cross. Whatever we see in the Exodus narrative of the God who saves, we see more fully in the cross of Christ. The death and resurrection of Jesus are the central events of salvation, bringing to fruition the promise-plan of God. The Exodus demonstrated the power and love of God before Moses, the Hebrew slaves, Pharaoh and his armies and the watching world: the cross stands at the centre of salvation history as the ultimate expression of the mission of God. The Exodus story became a powerful symbol in Israel's history, reminding generation after generation of Yahweh and all he had done: the cross is the central symbol of the Christian faith, communicating in the simplest possible form the actions of a saving God. What-

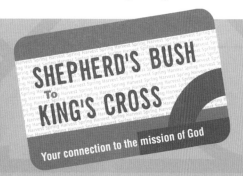

SHEPHERD'S BUSH
To
KING'S CROSS
Your connection to the mission of God

"Nothing can be certified as 'Christian' except it derive from Jesus; and the Church cannot represent itself as the Church of Christ if it does not come from him. The Church, its credibility and efficiency in our society, stand or fall according to whether it is the location and memorial of Jesus."
Hans Kung

ever else Christians are, they are people of the cross. Whatever else Christianity is or can be, it is always, and must always be, centred on the cross of Jesus.

The journey from Shepherd's Bush to King's Cross is a journey in God's plan of salvation. It is a journey on which we learn: ■

Salvation is reconciliation

The Hebrew slaves were not only set free *from* an oppressive relationship with Pharaoh, they were set free *into* a new relationship with Yahweh. The cross not only frees us from sin, it brings us into relationship with our Creator: it is a cross of reconciliation.

"To meet the penitent thief," Derek Tidball writes, "Jesus had to hang on the other cross beside him, but, when the man turned to him there, he did not say only 'Today I am with you on Calvary', but also 'Today you will be with me in paradise.' The sight of Jesus with us in our pain is the promise of our healing; the sight of Jesus sharing our death is the promise of our life."

[*The Message of the Cross*, p162]

The idea of salvation as reconciliation is clearly linked, in the New Testament, with the doctrine of *atonement*. We can be reconciled to God because Christ has taken our place, receiving in himself the death that was due to us and thereby demolishing the barrier that kept us from God. In 2 Corinthians 5:18–21, Paul uses the word reconciliation five times, before making the unique Christian claim that "God made him who had no sin to be sin for us, so that in him we might become the righteousness of God" [2 Cor 5:21].

Paul shows that "reconciliation is the divine act by which, on the basis of the death of Christ, God's holy displeasure against sinful man was appeased, the enmity between God and man was removed, and man was restored to proper relations with God. ... Reconciliation is not some polite ignoring or reduction of hostility but rather its total and objective removal. ... These

verses make it clear that God was the reconciler, that it was mankind that God reconciled to himself, although there is a sense in which this reconciliation was mutual; that Christ was God's agent in effecting reconciliation ("through Christ ... in Christ"); that the reconciliation has been accomplished ("reconciled ... was reconciling"); and that reconciliation involved the non-imputation of trespasses, i.e., forgiveness, which is complemented by the imputation of righteousness."

[*Expository Bible Commentary*] ■

Close Up:
The King's Cross can only fully make sense when we understand this central idea of substitution: that we receive salvation because Jesus took our place. Karl Barth writes that salvation asserts "there is a place which ought to be ours, that we ought to have taken this place, that we have been taken from it, that it is occupied by another, that this other acts in this place as only he can, in our cause and interest."

Salvation is victory

The deliverance of the Hebrew slaves was celebrated above all as the victory of God. God had gone to war against the powers of evil personified in Pharaoh's reign and he was victorious over them. The cross is the ultimate expression of God's victory over evil in the world.

'Until these days, evil forces have dominated our world – magic, evil spirits, superstition. But the coming of Jesus took them by surprise. ... God hoodwinked the powers of evil, outwitted them and defeated them by his own, silent wisdom, by three mysterious cries from the heart of the universe – birth, death, resurrection.'
Ignatius of Antioch

[Trans. David Winter – *After the Gospels*]

"By speaking of Jesus, Spirit and God in the same breath, the early disciple-community not only makes remarkable claims about Jesus within the monotheistic framework of Jewish thought, but, at the same time, makes staggering claims about God. The claim is not that Jesus is like God, but that God is like Jesus. Jesus, and especially Jesus in his crucifixion, is in some way the fullness of deity in human personhood. It is this claim that gave birth to the uniquely Christian belief that at the centre of all things there is a love that suffers."
Vinoth Ramachandra

SALVATION

Robert E. Webber writes of his recent rediscovery of the cross as 'the victory of Christ':

'In the Christian faith the key to the puzzle is the work of Jesus Christ. Once we have a solid grasp of the meaning of his work, the rest of the faith falls together around it. As far back as I can remember I was told that Christ was central to the Christian faith. However, when I began to reflect on the teaching I had received, I realised that the importance of Christ was always explained in terms of my personal salvation, little more. I have come to see through the study of the early Christian tradition that my view of Christ was severely limited. It wasn't that I didn't believe rightly. I simply didn't understand how far-reaching and all-inclusive Christ really was. When I discovered the universal and cosmic nature of Christ, I was given the key to a Christian way of viewing the whole world, a key that unlocked the door to a rich storehouse of spiritual treasures. ... The dominant interpretation of the work of Christ for the first thousand years of history is the proclamation that his death and resurrection constitute a victory over the powers of evil.'

[*Ancient Future Faith*, pp39, 43] ■

Salvation is decisive and final

When the waters of the miracle sea flowed back to drown Pharaoh's army, there was no question of a second opinion. God's victory was complete and final and for the people of Israel there was no going back. The cross of Christ stands similarly as decisive and final: it is a real event that makes a real difference. It does not merely *represent* or *symbolise* salvation, but delivers it once and for all.

'At the end of the nineteenth century, the great German dogmatic theologian Martin Kahler (1835–1912) posed a crucially important question to his academic contemporaries. Surveying the different ways the biblical doctrine of atonement had been interpreted since the days of the so-called European Enlightenment, Kahler asked: "Has Christ merely provided us with insights concerning an existing state of affairs, or has he actually brought about a new state of affairs? There is all the difference in the world between seeing Christ as, for instance, an 'icon of

God's grace' or a 'symbol of humanity's transcendence', and seeing Christ as establishing, through his death on the cross, a fundamentally new relationship between God and humanity."'
Vinoth Ramachandra
[*Faiths in Conflict?*, p132]

Salvation is not an incremental process of self-improvement – it is a decisive event that changes everything. "Given who God is and what human beings are," William Abraham writes, "it is conceptually odd in the extreme to say that one had been confronted with the rule of God but that life could go on as usual. The language of new birth, regeneration, acquittal, conversion, and the like is precisely what we should expect, and it is exactly what we find in the history of religious experience."

[*The Logic of Evangelism* (Grand Rapids: Eerdmans, 1989) pp121–122]

Vinoth Ramachandra points to the experience of the first Christians as evidence of this decisive and definitive change:

'Jesus was not remembered by the early disciples the way martyrs and sages from the past live on in the collective memory of a people. They did not make pilgrimages to the hill on which he was crucified or to the tomb in which his corpse was laid. Something had happened soon after Jesus' death that transformed a situation of defeat and desolation into one in which a new movement came into being, a movement that was characterized not by nostalgia but by "hope".'

[*Faiths in Conflict?*, p111] ■

Close Up:

In the New Testament it is the resurrection of Jesus that marks the decisive, unique and final victory of God: the resurrection is to Calvary what the crossing of the Red Sea is to the Passover: the final proof that the God who has promised salvation is uniquely ready and able to deliver on his promise. The resurrection is God's vindication of Jesus, confirming beyond argument the meaning of his birth, life and death.

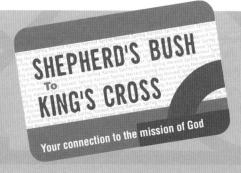

SHEPHERD'S BUSH
To
KING'S CROSS
Your connection to the mission of God

Salvation is unique and universal

At the heart of the election of Israel is God's affirmation that this is his chosen means of blessing the whole earth. There is no other plan; in that sense, the events of the Exodus are an essential part of the salvation that we, as Christians, enjoy. God has chosen to act in a particular way – and has made it the only way. So, too, the King's Cross is a unique and universal event. Unique because it is the only means by which God has chosen to liberate his creation: universal because it is for all. The cross of Jesus is the way by which all may come: but it is also the way by which all *must* come.

"This Christian claim is naturally offensive," Vinoth Ramachandra writes. "... but we must not suppose that this claim to universal validity is something that can quietly be removed from the Gospel without changing it into something entirely different from what it is. The mission of Jesus was limited to the Jews and did not look immediately beyond them; but his life, his methods and his message do not make sense, unless they are interpreted in the light of his own conviction that he was in fact the final and decisive work of God to men."

[*Faiths in Conflict?*, p116]

The uniqueness and universality of God's saving acts in Christ also fly in the face of the tolerant relativism of contemporary culture – the belief that all faiths and philosophies are ultimately valid in their own right, and that no claim to truth is universal.

'The issues raised for Christians in the West are particularly acute. Does tolerance require the abandonment of belief in universal truths? What is the distinctiveness of the Christian message in a world of many faiths? And what can Christians in the West learn from non-Western Christians and their struggle to live with integrity and faithfulness as minority communities?'
Vinoth Ramachandra
[*Faiths in Conflict?*, p11] ∎

The beneficiaries of salvation become its ambassadors

It is a consistent implication of God's saving acts in Exodus that there is no distinction between the *receivers* and the *carriers* of salvation: the calling of Israel is to fulfil both roles, as the two sides of the coin of salvation. The idea that it is possible to accept God's offer of salvation but to reject his call to mission seems to be unthinkable in the biblical narrative. It is *in the nature* of salvation that those who are saved become part of a new community bringing salvation to the world: this was

Close Up:

This belief that God has revealed a 'way of salvation' in Jesus that is at one and the same time for each person and for all – distinctive and definitive – leads Christians into significant questions of dialogue with other faiths. This will always be a difficult and challenging area, but never more so than in our newly globalised era in which the great faiths of the world share the same space as never before. An excellent example of the way in which dialogue and mission can be brought together is Chawkat Moucarry's *Faith to Faith – Christianity and Islam in Dialogue*. Moucarry is an Arab Christian, thoroughly established in his own faith and yet thoroughly open to all that can be gained from meaningful dialogue. He suggests,

'The teaching of Jesus contains no specific recommendations on debating with people of other faiths. However, what Jesus says about how to relate to people in general has special relevance: "So in everything, do to others what you would have them do to you, for this sums up the Law and the Prophets" (Matt 7:12). This command implies that Christians should have a fair attitude to Islam and Muslims. In practical terms, it means not comparing the ideals of Christianity with the reality of Islam, radical Muslims with moderate Christians, or mainstream Christianity with Islamic sects.'
[*Faith to Faith*, p17]

"The evangelistic harvest is always urgent. The destiny of men and of nations is always being decided. Every generation is strategic. We are not responsible for the past generation, and we cannot bear the full responsibility for the next one; but we do have our generation. God will hold us responsible as to how well we fulfil our responsibilities to this age and take advantage of our opportunities."
Billy Graham

SALVATION

true for the slaves freed at the Red Sea and it is true for the disciples freed at the King's Cross.

'Israel had experienced God's salvation in a way no other nation had. Therefore they had a missionary responsibility to be the priesthood of God among the nations.'
Chris Wright
[*Ambassadors to the World*, p32]

This same experience was repeated, as J B Phillips affirms, for the first Christians, "These early Christians (in the book of Acts) were led by the Spirit to the main task of bringing people to God through Christ, and were not permitted to enjoy fascinating sidetracks."

The involvement of people in mission cannot be seen as an afterthought to the main events of salvation: somehow it is wrapped up in the very heart of God's plan. From the very beginning, God has been moving towards the calling out of a people who would honour his name and carry his glory in the earth. Mission is part and parcel of salvation.

'The God of the Bible uses men and women to achieve his purposes. He has no need to do so. However, he humbly invites us to share with him in the fulfilling of his plans. What a remarkable privilege!'
Stephen Dray
[*Exodus, Free to serve*, p31] ■

Branch Lines

BRANCH LINE
Salvation as "shalom"

'Shalom is a comprehensive word, covering the manifold relationships of daily life, and expressing the ideal state of life in Israel. Its fundamental meaning is "totality", "wholeness", "well-being", "harmony", with stress on material prosperity untouched by violence or misfortune.'
Alan Richardson
[*A Theological Word Book of the Bible*, London: SCM, 1950, p165]

There is a strong link made in the biblical record between the idea of salvation and that of *wholeness*. Some of the language used of healing and health can also be translated as salvation, and words we translate *salvation* are often used to speak of healing and health. Because the biblical writers saw a human being as a whole person with physical, spiritual and social aspects, there is no rigid delineation of salvation as a purely spiritual concept. Thus wholeness – not just for the individual, but also for families, communities and the natural world – is part of what salvation means. The concept which best captures this overlap of salvation and wholeness is that of *shalom*, the Hebrew word for peace. Scholars are agreed that the word *shalom* means much more in the biblical context than does the term 'peace' today, and that these wider meanings are closely linked to the biblical understanding of salvation. Shalom is a picture of what God wants for the world – and therefore of what is obtained in salvation.

'Taking all the words used of healing, health and salvation together, we begin to obtain a nation of "wholeness" as meaning completeness, all-round health and life and strength, entailing freedom from evil in all our relationships.'
John P Baker
[*Salvation and Wholeness*, London: Fountain Trust, 1973, p17]

Shalom not only describes the benefits of salvation to be enjoyed by God's people, it also points to the nature of

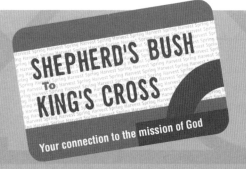

SHEPHERD'S BUSH
To
KING'S CROSS
Your connection to the mission of God

God's mission in the world. "The *shalom* culture," David Burnett writes, "was to be a witness to the nations by means of which they might see the glory of the Lord through his people. In this way other nations might be drawn to God, and enter into the blessing promised to Abraham. ... God is wanting his people in every generation to work out *shalom* in their own cultures, working for justice and freedom and ministering to the whole person."

[*God's Mission: Healing of the Nations*, Marc Europe / STL, 1986, p77]

Christian environmentalists rightly extend this wider meaning of salvation to include human interaction with the natural world. *The Care of Creation*, published by IVP in 2000, collects together a number of significant contributions in this growing field, and presents a compelling case for an understanding of mission that incorporates environmental action.

In *Creation Regained*, Al Wolters asserts that the whole creation is involved in God's promise-plan.

"Virtually all of the basic words describing salvation in the Bible imply a *return* to an originally good state or situation," he writes. "These terms suggest a *restoration* of some good thing that was spoiled or lost. Acknowledging this scriptural emphasis, theologians have sometimes spoken of salvation as "re-creation" – not to imply that God scraps his earlier creation and in Jesus Christ makes a new one, but rather to suggest that he hangs on to his fallen original creation and *salvages* it. He refuses to abandon the work of his hands – in fact he sacrifices his own son to save his original project."

[*Creation Regained*]

The King who gives his life on the cross has not come for his own purposes, but on behalf of the Creator. The cross is the fulfilment of every covenant promise God has made – going back not just to Moses or Abraham, but to Noah and his family and, before them, to the garden itself and the lost relationship with Adam and Eve.

'Since the cosmos itself is in bondage, depressed under evil forces, the essential content of the word "salvation" is that the world itself will be rescued, or renewed, or set free. Salvation is a cosmic event affecting the whole of creation. It is not simply the internal renewal of man's religious attitude. ... Salvation is not simply the overcoming of my rebellion and the forgiveness of my guilt, but salvation is the liberation of the whole world process of which I am only a small part.'
J. Kallas

[*The Satanward View: A Study in Pauline Theology* (Philadelphia: Westminster, 1966), p74] ■

BRANCH LINE
Salvation as story

One of the things God told the Hebrews to do was to tell to their children the stories of their community – how they came into being and how God freed them at the Red Sea. These stories were to be foundational to the lives and faith of the children as they grew. If children were not told the stories of their tribe and all that God had done for them, how would they know who they were and how they should live? Telling the story, remembering all that God had done, passing on the story to the next generation: these were the survival tactics of the community of Israel.

This is also, according to Walter Brueggemann, a responsibility of the Christian community.

'Evangelism is indeed to do again and again what Jews and Christians have always done, to tell "the old, old story" but to do so in ways that impact every aspect of our contemporary life, public and personal.'
[*Biblical Perspectives on Evangelism*, p11]

Not only must the story be told, but it must be translated and 'inculturated' into the time and context of each new generation, continuing the emphasis of incarnation:

"Where Jesus is, there is life, the synoptic Gospels tell us. There sick life is healed, saddened life is given fresh heart, marginalized life is accepted, captive life is freed, and the tormenting spirits of death are driven out. For since his baptism God's Spirit has 'rested' on Jesus and acts through him. ... The mission of Jesus and the mission of the Spirit are nothing other than movements of life: movements of healing, of liberation, of righteousness and justice. Jesus didn't bring a new religion into the world. What he brought was new life."
Jurgen Moltmann

SALVATION

'The incarnation itself gives us the model of relevance. God shows up on our turf speaking our language so that we might understand.'
Mike Riddell, Mark Pierson, Cathy Kirkpatrick
[*The Prodigal Project* (SPCK, 2000)] ■

Close Up:

The telling of the gospel story involves more than words – it is a living out of salvation: embodying the message of God in the life of his people.
Michael Nazir-Ali writes: "The gospel is not a dis-embodied message that can be hawked from culture to culture. It is incarnate in people's lifestyle, relationships and values. It is this 'embodied' faith that encounters and transforms cultures, while, at the same time, remaining dynamic itself; this inherent translatability makes the mission of the church universal."
[*Shapes of the Church to Come*, p17]

But we cannot duck the fact that words have a central part to play in the fulfilment of this calling. The story must be told. Walter Brueggemann writes: "At the centre of the act of evangelism is the message announced, a verbal, out-loud assertion of something decisive not known until this moment of utterance. There is no way that anyone, including an embarrassed liberal, can avoid this lean, decisive assertion which is at the core of evangelism."
[*Biblical Perspectives on Evangelism*, p14]

▶ BRANCH LINE
Salvation as participation – "I was there"

The telling of the Exodus story in each new Hebrew generation involved more than remembering – it involved participation. Terence E. Fretheim notes: "The Jewish liturgy for Passover (*Passover Haggadah*) stresses that worshippers in every celebration are actual participants in God's saving deed: God brought us out of Egypt."
[*Interpretation: Exodus*, p139]

To belong to God's people is to say 'I was there.' Contemporary Jewish writer David Grossman says: "Even today, the Jewish people read in the *Passover Haggadah* that 'in every generation, each individual is bound to regard himself as if he personally had gone forth from 'Egypt'."
[*The Second Book of Moses, Called Exodus*, Canongate Books Ltd, Great Britain 1998, p xi]

Bill Muir, author of *Three Story Evangelism*, quotes an incident from the life of the painter Rembrandt in order to apply the same thinking to Christian experience:
When Rembrandt completed his great portrait of the crucifixion, he called some of his friends over to see his latest masterpiece... When they looked over into the corner of the painting, there was a man who looked like Rembrandt. One of his friends said, "You know, that fellow looking up at the cross looks just like you." Rembrandt very sombrely said to his friend, "It is me. I was there. That cross was for me."' ■

▶ FELLOW TRAVELLERS

Three Story Evangelism
Bill Muir, of Youth for Christ in America, has developed an approach to evangelism around the model of three stories. He suggests that personal Christian witness is an overlap of three distinct stories:
> Your story
> My Story
> God's Story

I cannot expect you to listen either to my story or God's story until I have been willing to listen to your story – listening is the first stage of evangelism. Then, I cannot expect you to grasp abstract concepts of God unless they are grounded in experience and reality – 'my story' puts flesh on the Christian gospel. Lastly, I cannot expect you to meet with God without knowing who he is and what he has done – God's story is the key to unlocking your life. Personal witness consists of listening to

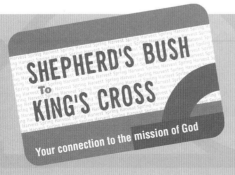

SHEPHERD'S BUSH
To
KING'S CROSS
Your connection to the mission of God

your story and sharing my story and the way it has been touched by God's story.

The God Who Answers by Love

The road ended not only in the bitterness of apparent failure, not only in the physical torment of a cruel and gruesome death, but in the spiritual darkness of separation from God, bearing upon himself the sins of the world. That is how the world was redeemed; not by Elijah and the Messiah coming and ridding Israel of her political foes, calling down fire to burn up all opposition, but by Jesus, commissioned by John in the spirit and power of Elijah ridding Israel and the world of her true enemies. Just as Elijah challenged the powers of darkness to that great contest, in which the god who answers by fire was to be God, so now Jesus takes on the rulers of the world: the might of Rome, the law of Israel, and behind both the usurping and destroying power of Satan. And this time the rules of the contest are: the god who answers by love, let him be God.

Tom Wright

[*Crown and Fire*, p45] ■

APPLICATIONS

The Everywhere Cross

Justin Martyr wrote, in the second century:

'The sign of the cross is all around all the time. The mast of a ship carries it – the cross formed by the yardarm is like a symbol of victory as the boat drives ahead through stormy seas. Ploughs and spades bear the cross shape. For that matter, human beings are distinguished from animals by standing upright and being able to extend their arms like a cross. Even the badges of power in our society express the idea of the cross in powerful symbolism. When the Roman legions march behind their ensign, they are in fact marching under a cross, and when victory poles are carried, the victory of which they remind us is the victory of the cross. So, if we wish, we may see the Lord Christ in everything: his victory in every human

symbol, his glory in every earthly kingdom, his sign in every heathen inscription.'

David Winter

[*After the Gospels*, p74]

● How might it impact your life if, every time you saw a cross 'hidden' in the ordinary things of life, you stopped to reflect on the victory of Christ?

Assessing Shalom?

Mark Greene suggests the following exercise as a means of measuring your HFQ – 'Human Flourishing Quotient'. Score yourself on a scale of 1 to 10 (10 is 'yes' and great; 1 is 'no' and awful).

1 My relationship with God is flourishing, and I get about the right amount of time with him.
2 I get about the right amount of time for family/key relationships.
3 I get about the right amount of sleep.
4 I get about the right amount of time for rest.
5 I get to do things that refresh me reasonably often.
6 My lifestyle allows me to stay reasonably healthy.
7 I get about the right amount of time for church life.
8 I work about the right amount of time.
9 I'm reasonably satisfied with the structure of my life.
10 I feel that there's another Christian who knows me, to whom I can open up my life.

[*Thank God it's Monday*, p81] ■

"Christ comes to the cross as the fireman comes to the fire, as the lifeboat comes to the sinking ship, as the rescue team comes to the wounded man in the Alpine snow. They have what it takes to help and deliver, but they must come to where the fire burns, the storm rages, the avalanche entombs and makes themselves vulnerable to the danger that such a coming involves."
Derek Tidball

SALVATION

CONNECTIONS
The Matrix
(Warner Bros 1999)

Summary

Computer hacker Neo feels that not all is right with the world. He meets rebel leader Morpheus who tells him that he's actually a slave. Morpheus gives Neo a pill that will enable Neo to see the truth at last – he is cocooned in a pod along with billions of other people. While their bodies are used as an energy source by 'intelligent' machines that run the world, their brains are connected to a computer simulation of 'reality' – The Matrix.

Once freed, Neo has to relearn the basic nature of his existence. This is a difficult transition for Neo. Morpheus explains: "We never free a mind once it's reached a certain age. It's dangerous, the mind has trouble letting go."

Freedom and salvation are positive concepts. The world longs for freedom, and Christians are no exception. Neo has hard choices to make before he can experience freedom. His salvation depends in part on him recognising the truth. Is our twenty-first century world in a similar position? What does the Bible say about freedom, and is it relevant? How does the Bible picture salvation as freedom? ■

Bible Study

1 Slavery
You are a slave, Neo. Like everyone else you were born into bondage, born into a prison that you cannot smell or taste or touch – a prison for your mind. (Morpheus)

● Read John 8:31–41. From what did Jesus think his hearers needed freeing? Why didn't they see their need for freedom?

NOTE: Jesus' hearers claimed that they had never been slaves – they evidently thought that he was talking about political freedom (from the Romans). Jesus makes it clear that he is talking about spiritual freedom (v34). Central to understanding this passage is an idea of son-ship which was important in their culture (and still is in many rural parts of the world today) – a son does what his father does. So, a fisherman's son becomes a fisher-man and so on. Jesus uses this idea to tell his hearers that they don't act like the one they claim as their father (Abraham) so they are not his children. Instead, they do what Satan does and what they have heard from him, so demonstrating that they are his children.

● Read Romans 6:16–23. What does it mean to be a slave to sin? What are the consequences of being a slave to sin?

2 Choice
I'm trying to free your mind, Neo, but I can only show you the door. You're the one that has to walk through it. You have to let it all go, Neo – fear, doubt and disbelief. Free – your – mind. (Morpheus)

● Read John 8:37–47. What choice did the people have to make? How does this choice show itself in our actions?

● Read Romans 6:8–14. What does it mean to die with Christ? How do we count ourselves dead to sin?

Implications
You have to understand, most of these people are not ready to be unplugged. And many of them are so inert, so hopelessly dependent on the system that they will fight to protect it. (Morpheus)

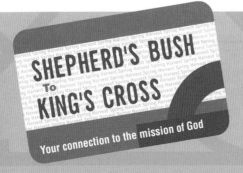

- Jesus promises us the truth. The truth is not always what we want to hear. How, then, can it lead us to freedom?

- How would you describe the benefits of the freedom Jesus offers to someone who had not experienced it yet? What do you think would be the most appealing aspect?

From *Connect Bible Studies: What does the Bible say about... The Matrix*. ISBN 1 85999 579 9 published online by Damaris, and in print by Scripture Union – Linking the Word to the World. www.connectbiblestudies.com – these studies are available to buy from this site. ■

 # THE BOOK STALL

Rose Dowsett, Thinking Clearly About The Great Commission, Monarch

Stephen Travis, The Bible as a Whole, Bible Reading Fellowship

Andrew Lord, Spirit, Kingdom and Mission: A Charismatic Missiology, Grove Booklets

Andreas J. Köstenberger & Peter T. O'Brien, Salvation to the Ends of the Earth, Apollos IVP

Derek Tidball, The Message of The Cross, IVP

Walter Brueggemann, Biblical Perspectives on Evangelism, Abingdon Press

Vinoth Ramachandra, Faiths in Conflict?, IVP

FREEDOM

1 DESTINATIONS AND DEFINITIONS
Freedom

freedom *noun* **1** the condition of being free to act, move, etc without restriction. **2** personal liberty or independence, eg from slavery, serfdom, etc. **3** a right or liberty • *freedom of speech* • *freedom to demonstrate*. **4** (often **freedom from something**) the state of being without or exempt from something • *freedom from pain*. **5** autonomy, self-government or independence, eg of a state or republic. **6** unrestricted access to or use of something • *give someone the freedom of one's house*. **7** honorary citizenship of a place, entitling one to certain privileges • *was granted freedom of the town of Rochester*. **8** frankness; candour. **9** over-familiarity; presumptuous behaviour. **ETYMOLOGY:** Anglo-Saxon *freodom*

free *adj* (*freer*, *freest*) **1** allowed to move as one pleases; not shut in. **2** not tied or fastened. **3** allowed to do as one pleases; not restricted, controlled or enslaved. **4** said of a country: independent. **5** costing nothing. **6** open or available to all. **7** not working, busy, engaged or having another appointment. **8** not occupied; not being used. **9** said of a translation: not precisely literal. **10** smooth and easy • *free and relaxed body movement*. **11** without obstruction • *given free passage*. **12** *derog* said of a person's manner: disrespectful, over-familiar or presumptuous. **13** *chem* not combined with another chemical element. **14** *in compounds* **a** not containing the specified ingredient, substance, factor, etc (which is usually considered to be undesirable) • *sugar-free* • *milk-free* • *nuclear-free*; **b** free from, or not affected or troubled by, the specified thing • *trouble-free meeting* • *stress-free weekend* • *carefree*; **c** not paying or exempt from the specified thing • *rent-free* • *tax-free* A 17c and particularly since the 1970s in sense 14a; 16c in sense 14b; Anglo-Saxon in sense 14c. *adverb* **1** without payment • *free of charge*. **2** freely; without restriction • *wander free*. *verb* (*frees*, *freed*, *freeing*) to allow someone to move without restriction after a period in captivity, prison, etc; to set or make someone free; to liberate someone. **freely** *adverb*. **freeness** *noun*. **feel free** *colloq* you have permission (to do something) • *Feel free to borrow my bike anytime*. **for free** *colloq* without

payment. **free and easy** cheerfully casual or tolerant. a **free hand** scope to choose how best to act. **free of** or **from something** without; not or no longer having or suffering (especially something harmful, unpleasant or not wanted) • *free of fear* • *finally free from the aching pain*. **free with something** open, generous, lavish or liberal • *free with her money* • *free with his body*. **it's a free country** *colloq* there's no objection to acting in the way mentioned. **make free with something** to make too much, or unacceptable, use of something not one's own. **ETYMOLOGY:** Anglo-Saxon *freo*

God is the liberator who breaks the power of slavery and ends the oppression of his people. Exodus is a story of freedom... ■

2 DISTRICT LINE
'Let my people go!'

'"Let my people go"... with this cry, Moses demanded that his people be released from slavery. "Let go" is a call for liberation. From that time on, liberation has been the central theme of God's redeeming work.'
Harvey Perkins
[Cited in David Burnett, *God's Mission: Healing of the Nations*, p62]

'God is the champion of the poor and those pushed to the margins of life; God is one who liberates them from the Pharaohs of this world.'
Terence E. Fretheim
[*Interpretation: Exodus*, p18]

Whatever else the Exodus story contains, it is without doubt a story of freedom. Beginning with a slave people trapped beyond help under a cruel and oppressive regime, it ends with a people liberated and self-determining, formed into a nation and free to worship their God. Exodus is a narrative of liberation. Not surprisingly, it has been a symbol and beacon of freedom for much of recorded history.

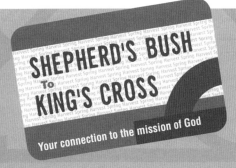

SHEPHERD'S BUSH To KING'S CROSS
Your connection to the mission of God

"Much of our praying is just asking God to bless some folks that are ill, and to keep us plugging along. But prayer is not merely prattle, it is warfare."
Alan Redpath

At the height of the English civil war, Oliver Cromwell is said to have described the Exodus as 'the only parallel of God's dealing with us that I know in the world'. Similarly, Martin Luther King Jr. frequently presented the struggles of the civil rights movement in 1960s America in Exodus language. On the day before he was shot by an assassin in 1968, he said:

'I've been to the mountaintop. ... And I've looked over. And I've seen the promised land. I may not get there with you, but I want you to know tonight that we as a people will get to the promised land. And I'm happy tonight. I'm not worried about anything. I'm not fearing any man. Mine eyes have seen the glory of the coming of the Lord.'

The inspiration of Exodus becomes particularly pronounced where there is a protracted struggle for liberation – as there was in both the examples cited above. Freedom does not come easily, nor is it cheap, and a central section of the Exodus story recounts what can only be described as a battle for freedom. It is not the slaves who fight – this is not a people's revolution – but God who fights for them. The battle has five distinct phases:

- The initial confrontation with Pharaoh and the cry of "Let my people go!" in which God signals his intention to liberate the slaves – and offers Pharaoh a peaceful way out. [Exod 5:1–6:13]
- The confrontation between Moses and Aaron and the Egyptian magicians in which, behind closed doors, God's superior power is demonstrated. [Exod 6:28–7:13]
- A series of nine plagues or signs of increasing magnitude, in which the whole natural order of Egyptian life is disrupted at God's intervention. [Exod 7:14–10:29]
- A tenth and final plague touching the Egyptians themselves, and leading to the Passover and the 'night-flight' of the slaves. [Exod 11:1–12:39]
- The crossing of the Red Sea, at which God's victory over Pharaoh's army is full and final: the people of Israel are at last free. [Exod 14:5–29]

At each of these phases the battle intensifies, and many times Pharaoh seems ready to relent, only to harden his heart and fight on. Only when the final battle has been won, when Pharaoh's army has been destroyed and the waters of the Red Sea stand between the tyrant and his former slaves, does he finally capitulate.

The picture of God at war, head-to-head against Pharaoh for the prize of his people's freedom, offers a number of important insights into the biblical understanding of liberation:
- **biblical liberation brings freedom from oppression**: the struggle has a political and social dimension as Yahweh goes to war against the ungodly exploitation Pharaoh's regime imposes.
- **biblical liberation brings freedom from evil**: behind the surface struggle there is a spiritual battle as Yahweh takes issue with the gods of Egypt.
- **biblical liberation brings freedom from death**: the ultimate battle is for the creation itself, as Yahweh does battle for life and against death in the world he has made.

The plague narratives of Exodus are not easy to understand for contemporary, Western readers. The intensity of this battle – and the resulting damage and loss of life – do not sit easily with our worldview. But they are an important measure of the reality and intensity of this war.

Whatever else this story says to us, it tells us, in all three of the dimensions cited above, that the battle is real. This is no phoney war: God is not engaged in a public relations exercise. There is real evil in the world, and the price of freedom is real. Whether the enemies we confront are social, political or spiritual, they will not give up their power without a fight. The call to follow Yahweh, and his Christ, is a call to war. ■

The first commandment ever given by God to humanity begins with the words "You are free..."
Genesis 2:16

FREEDOM

Main Lines
God at War?

MAIN LINE 1
Freedom from oppression

'Egypt symbolised evil in the form of humiliating oppression, ungodly exploitation, and crushing domination.'
Martin Luther King Jr.
[*Strength to Love*]

'Whenever men by their own fault or by some superior power have come under the control of someone else, and have lost their freedom to implement their will and decisions, and when their own resources are inadequate to deal with that other power, they can regain their freedom only by the intervention of a third party.'
Colin Brown
[*Redemption*]

There can be no question that the Exodus narrative has a significant political and social dimension. The predicament of the slaves is real: their oppression is concrete, and their sufferings are in the physical and social realm. They are in a life-threatening situation, the victims of a campaign of ethnic genocide. In this context, Yahweh clearly sides with the oppressed against the oppressor, with the weak against the strong.

'[He is] a God who takes sides. God is God of the oppressed; God enters into their difficult, suffering situations to set things right. God is a God who is concerned to move people from slavery to freedom.'
Terence E. Fretheim
[*Interpretation: Exodus*, p31]

In the twentieth century, the link between the mission of God and the liberation of the oppressed has been developed in Liberation Theology, explored more fully in the Branch Line below. But this recent development should not be seen as unprecedented: throughout the biblical record, and through church history, the thread of liberation is evident.

'The God we know in the Bible, is a liberating God ... a God who intervenes in history in order to break down structures of injustice and who raises up prophets in order to point out the way of justice.'
Emilio Castro
[Cited in Roger Sainsbury, *Justice on the Agenda*, p12]

Gary Haugen, who was director of the UN genocide investigation in Rwanda, recently suggested that the church needs to recover this 'liberating' dimension of faith and mission:

'As Christians we have learned much about sharing the love of Christ with people all over the world who have never heard the gospel. We continue to see the salvation message preached in the far corners of the earth and to see indigenous Christian churches vigorously extending Christ's kingdom on every continent. We have learned how to feed the hungry, heal the sick and shelter the homeless. But there is one thing we haven't learned to do, even though God's Word repeatedly calls us to the task. We haven't learned how to rescue the oppressed. ... Somewhere during the twentieth century some of us have simply stopped believing that God can actually use us to answer the prayers of children, women and families who suffer under the hand of abusive power or authority in their communities. We sit in the same paralysis of despair as those who don't even claim to know a Saviour – and in some cases, we manifest even less hope.'
[*Good News About Injustice*, IVP, 1999, p72] ■

MAIN LINE 2
Freedom from evil

'The contest between Egypt and Israel, Pharaoh and Moses, was a contest not only of strength but of spiritual power.'
Derek Tidball
[*The Message of the Cross*, p59]

To read Exodus only in terms of political and social liberation is to ignore key aspects of it and miss its meaning. Though social liberation is present in the

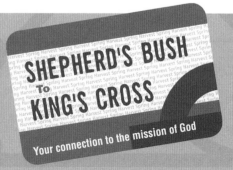

"Jesus Christ, God's Son, became a slave, that we who were spiritually enslaved might become sons. Are we living like slaves or like sons?"
Mark Stibbe

story, it is not the end of the story. This is a narrative of spiritual warfare – of God's cosmic campaign against the forces of evil. The public realities of liberation are matched by the hidden realities of God's spiritual work: just as the Exodus event itself could not have happened without the Passover:

"The transformation of the sovereign action of God on behalf of Israel into a common metaphor for any movement towards freedom is dangerous," Derek Tidball warns. "Too often people want the Exodus without the Passover, liberation without the blood, salvation without the sacrifice and freedom without the cross. In the historic understanding of Israel, the Exodus and the Passover are inseparable. The one would not have happened without the other."
[The Message of the Cross, p51]

This spiritual battle, in which God confronts and ultimately defeats the hidden powers of evil in the world, lies behind every aspect of God's mission.

✦ It is consistently present in the ministry of Jesus
Derek Tidball finds overwhelming evidence in the Gospel of Mark for the reality of spiritual conflict at the heart of Jesus' ministry:

'People needed to be saved from slavery to sin and from Satan, whose handiwork was everywhere to be seen, creating havoc and destroying lives. In a typically breathtaking passage, 4:35–5:43, Mark gives us a taste of the need for emancipation. Jesus delivers his disciples from the destructive forces of a fallen nature, a man from the disintegrating forces of demonic possession, a woman from the degrading impact of a crippling disease and a family from the devastating force of the final enemy, death. Elsewhere it is the enslaving rules of the religious leaders, or the corrupting forces of sin lurking within their own natures, or even the captivating seduction of materialism from which people need to be emancipated. The whole of Mark's Gospel cries out for a*

liberator. People were oppressed, and by more than the might of Rome.'
[The Message of the Cross, p139]

"A warfare worldview," Gregory Boyd writes, "is at the centre of Jesus' understanding of his mission, and therefore of his understanding of the kingdom of God."
[God at War, p192]

Ultimately the battle finds its focus in the cross, where Jesus finally confronts and disarms the powers of evil. The cross is "the locus of a cosmic battle, in which Jesus achieves a decisive victory over Satan."
Gregory Boyd
[God at War, p230]

"This brilliant victory over the rebel powers through the foolishness of the cross," Boyd writes, "stands at the centre of everything the New Testament is about."
[God at War, p259]

✦ It lies behind Christian social action and the struggle for justice
Whilst many Christians see spiritual warfare at work in evangelism, discipleship and church growth, they often fail to recognise it in social action and work amongst the poor. Bryant L Myers of World Vision insists that here, too, there is a hidden battle. He cites theologian Jayakumar Christian as saying:

'It is not simply human beings, and the systems within which they live, that create and sustain poverty. There is a cosmic adversary who is working against life. This adversary is "a liar and the father of lies" (John 8:44). Any account of poverty that ignores the reality of an Evil One lacks the full explanatory power that the Bible offers.'
[Walking with the Poor, p75]

"Social action is a confrontation with the powers that be," Melba Maggay writes. "We are, ultimately, not battling against flesh and blood, nor merely dismantling

"The category of liberation is biblical and has resonance within the modern consciousness. All over the world people are asking to be free of want, tyranny and oppression."
Clark Pinnock and Robert C Brow

FREEDOM

unjust social systems; we are confronting the powers in their cosmic and social dimensions."

[Cited in Bryant L Myers, *Walking with the Poor*, p86]

✦ It is an important aspect of the calling and mission of the church

In the New Testament, the calling and role of the church is expressed in the same spiritual warfare language as the ministry of Jesus. The very existence of the church is evidence of the defeat of Satan.

"We who used to be captives of the satanic kingdom are now the very ones who proclaim its demise," Gregory Boyd asserts. "The church is, as it were, God's eternal 'trophy case' of grace – we eternally exist 'to the praise of his glorious grace' (Eph 1:6; cf v12) – and we are this because we evidence God's brilliance and power in bringing about the destruction of his foes, and thus the liberation of his people."

[*God At War*, p252]

The church's understanding of its role, and of God's mission in the world, is impoverished where this awareness of the spiritual war is lost. The *1993 Statement of Spiritual Warfare from the Intercession Working Group of the Lausanne Committee on World Evangelisation* includes this statement: "We wondered if the time we have had the gospel in the West has made us less conscious of the powers of darkness in recent centuries. We noted also that the influence of the Enlightenment in our education, which traces everything to natural causes, has further dulled our consciousness of the powers of darkness." ■

In Brief:

Spiritual warfare is essential to the very existence of the church, is part of its nature and role and is indispensable in the fulfilment of its calling and mission.

MAIN LINE 3
Freedom from death

If the liberation of the Hebrew slaves represents God's battle for freedom in terms both of political oppression and spiritual war, it also points to an even bigger picture: it is a battle for the freedom of the creation itself.

"The most basic perspective within which the plagues are to be understood is a theology of creation," Terence E. Fretheim writes. "Pharaoh's oppressive, anti-life measures against Israel are anticreational, striking at the point where God was beginning to fulfil the creational promise of fruitfulness in Israel (Gen 1:28; Exod 1:7) ... The theological grounding for the plagues is an understanding of the moral order, created by God for the sake of justice and well-being in the world. Pharaoh's moral order is bankrupt, severely disrupting this divine intent, and hence he becomes the object of the judgement inherent in God's order."

[*Interpretation: Exodus*, p106, 110]

In this view, Pharaoh is seen as a force of death, resisting and frustrating God's life-giving plans for his creation.

'Pharaoh is seen to be both a human being and an embodiment of cosmic forces working against God's creational designs.'
Terence E. Fretheim
[*Interpretation: Exodus*, p19]

The battle focuses on the plight of the Hebrew slaves, but represents the much larger conflict, in which God's life-giving plans confront the forces and fruits of death, 'the last enemy' [I Cor 15:26].

"The Evil One is in the world working actively against life and shalom. This evil works through the sin in human beings, encouraging bad choices by promoting a web of lies.'
Bryant L Myers
[*Walking with the Poor*, p122]

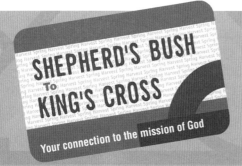

SHEPHERD'S BUSH
To
KING'S CROSS
Your connection to the mission of God

"Those who have ears. Those who have cares. Those who have fears. Those who have tears. Let them hear... and see... and feel... and breathe."
Mike Riddell

Both the Old and New Testaments, Vinoth Ramachandra writes, are "filled with descriptions of how Yahweh-Adonai, the covenant God of Israel, is waging war against those forces which try to thwart and subvert his plans for his creation. He battles against those false gods which human beings have fashioned from the created world, idolised and used for their own purpose ... He contends against every form of social injustice and pulls off every cloak under which it seeks to hide."

[*Faiths in Conflict?*, p97]

In Brief:

Because the battle is for the whole creation, the victory of God – expressed in the Exodus and ultimately in Jesus – holds the promise of freedom not only for those immediately implicated, but for the whole cosmos.

'The good news is that with the victory of Yahweh, all creation is now freed (as it had been groaning in travail like slaves in Egypt); all creation is now authorised, to be its best true self, functioning as intended by the Creator who is creation's best guard and guarantor. The news assures that the power of the gods of death has been decisively broken.'

Walter Brueggemann

[*Biblical Perspectives on Evangelism*, p31]

This was the view of the early Christians, who made a strong connection between the victory of the risen Christ and their own struggles with evil in society. Robert Webber points out that:

'Classical Christianity affirms the centrality of Christ to all creation and offers a distinct way to deal with the problem of evil. It sees the presence and power of evil in society as the impact of original sin, which permeates all the structures of existence.'

[*Ancient Future Faith*, p41]

Citing Romans 8:19-21, Andrew Lord sees in the work of Christ the promise that "the whole of creation will be brought together in glorious freedom."

[*Spirit, Kingdom and Mission*, p10]

The liberating God – whose cry at the Shepherd's Bush, "Let my people go" becomes the cry at the King's Cross, "It is finished" – has won the ultimate battle against Satan and the forces of evil and death. He now claims the ultimate prize: a cosmos delivered from evil and free to the very core of its being. ■

Branch Lines

BRANCH LINE
The bondage breaker

Moses' plans to return to Egypt and confront Pharaoh are interrupted by a bizarre event "at a lodging place" on the journey. Here "the LORD met Moses and was about to kill him" [Exod 4:24]. Moses' life is saved by his wife Zipporah, who circumcises their son, causing God to relent. Commentators agree that this is a strange passage in the text, but that it refers to removing compromise from the family. Moses had failed to circumcise his son, which was the accepted sign of covenant obedience.

"Thus for one small neglect," the Expository Bible Commentary explains, "apparently out of deference for his wife's wishes, or perhaps to keep peace in the home, Moses almost forfeited his opportunity to serve God and wasted eighty years of preparation and training!"

The event serves to illustrate the extreme seriousness of the battle to which God has called Moses:

'This is a divine demonstration of the seriousness of the matter upon which God and Moses are about to embark: a life-and-death struggle in which Israel's very life will be imperilled.'

Terence E. Fretheim

[*Interpretation: Exodus*, p81]

"If you love someone: set them free"
Sting

"The pursuit of Christ is a pilgrimage that involves learning how to give up power for the sake of others. It produces a freedom from fear and anxiety, so that followers can relinquish the need for control."
Mike Riddell

FREEDOM

There is a personal dimension to spiritual warfare that we ignore at our peril. No matter how focused we are on political and social liberation, it means nothing unless we ourselves are set free. Freedom, in the Bible, is personal as well as public.

Neil Anderson, of Freedom in Christ Ministries, has written extensively of this personal dimension of God's liberation. "Being alive and free in Christ is part of positional sanctification, which is the basis for progressive sanctification," he writes in *The Bondage Breaker*. "In other words, we are not trying to become children of God, we are children of God who are becoming like Christ."

Freedom, he says, is part of the package. He suggests that there is an authority inherent in the word of God that the believer must take hold of, if they are to experience the fullness of personal liberation. Fighting the enemy of God is not a question of techniques but of truth, carried not in weapons but in words:

'You don't have to outshout him or outmuscle him to be free of his influence. You just have to out-truth him. Believe, declare, and act upon the truth of God's Word, and you will thwart Satan's strategy.'

[*The Bondage Breaker*, p25]

Personal freedom, Boyd asserts, is at the very heart of salvation: "One of the most frequent and fundamental ways in which the New Testament depicts our salvation as a freeing consequence of Christ's cosmic victory over Satan is by referring to it as 'redemption'. The root of this term *lytron* means a 'ransom' or 'price of release', and the term 'redemption' (*aploytrōsis*) was almost a technical term in the ancient world for the purchase or manumission of a slave. As applied to believers in the New Testament, it implies that our salvation consists fundamentally in being freed from a form of slavery."

[*God at War*, p265] ■

BRANCH LINE
The liberation of theology?

'You work with a family in a city where the husband was picked up by the police a month ago. You try to find out where he is, or even if he is alive. Then it happens again and again, until you realise that you face not only a pastoral problem but an organised repression which must be resisted. You work with peasants seeking food until you realise that the food lands are all tied up in plantations and latifundias (landed estates) which produce non-food crops such as coffee and sugar for export to rich countries. You realise that the problem is not lack of food or land but the way in which it is owned and distributed.'
Paul Marshall

[*Thine is the Kingdom*, Basingstoke: Marshall, Morgan and Scott, 1984, p73]

Liberation Theology is a global movement of the late twentieth century that first emerged amongst Roman Catholic activists in Latin America in the 1960s and 1970s. "Theologians and priests, many of them from Europe," Paul Marshall explains, "found themselves among people in deep poverty and misery, in societies with vast disparities of wealth, and political regimes which existed to maintain this situation rather than to seek justice."

[*Thine is the Kingdom*, p73]

Associated with a Peruvian priest, a Mexican academic and a Uruguayan Jesuit (Gustavo Gutierrez, Jose Porfirio Miranda, and Juan Luis Segundo), the ideas of Liberation Theology have gone on to influence both Catholic and Protestant theologians in many parts of the world. The shooting in 1980 of Oscar Romero, who as archbishop of San Salvador had become an outspoken public advocate of liberation, drew the world's attention to the significance of this theology.

The Exodus narrative has been a foundational text for the theologians of liberation, inspiring them to believe that God can act now as he acted then: to free oppressed people from their slavery. The movement has

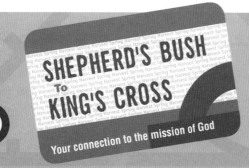

"This preaching of the gospel can never be irrelevant. But if the church which preaches it is not living corporately a life which corresponds with it, is living a comfortable cohabitation with the powers of this age, is failing to challenge the powers of darkness and to manifest in its life the power of the living Lord to help and to heal, then by its life it closes the doors which its preaching would open."
Lesslie Newbigin

broadened out to include many issues of economics, race and gender, but in essence its main tenets remain those articulated by Gustavo Gutierrez. Tony Lane summarises the five key aspects of Gutierrez's theology as:

- It makes no claim to be a universal theology – in fact it rejects such a possibility. It is a Latin American theology in response to the Latin American situation.
- It looks to the liberation of theology – offering a whole new way of doing theology as 'a critical reflection on Christian praxis in the light of the word'.
- It begins with an analysis of the way things are in concrete terms – in this case a Marxist analysis of the struggles of the poor in Latin America.
- It re-visits the major themes of Christian theology in the light of this analysis and commitment – so salvation is associated with the political liberation of the poor. No distinction is allowed between sacred and secular history – God is at work in the history of the real world to work out his plan of salvation.
- It looks to a re-reading of the Bible in support of its claim – especially the Exodus, which is interpreted as a political liberation – in fact the self-liberation of the Hebrew slaves. The over-spiritualization of the Bible is rejected in favour of a more earthy, real-world hermeneutic.

Tony Lane

[*The Lion Concise History of Christian Thought*]

Many commentators – both Catholic and Protestant – have rejected Liberation Theology because of its association with Marxism, its emphasis on political action at the expense of 'spiritual' realities and its implication that the poor are 'blessed of God' simply by the fact of being poor: but many, too, have valued the insights of this significant movement.

Michael Nazir-Ali, in *Shapes of the Church to Come*, affirms that "the various liberation theologies, as they have emerged in different parts of the world, have moved our understanding of the poor as objects of compassion to the need for justice for them and further to the poor themselves being the agents of the change God wants to bring about in the world."

[*Shapes of Church to Come*, p63]

"It is all too easy for those from a traditional school of theological thought to brush aside what is being said by liberation theologians without listening to what they are actually saying," David Burnett writes. "They are concerned with the oppression of the poor by the rich, frequently a concern that the Christian church has ignored. But the Exodus reveals to us that God is concerned about the poor and the oppressed, and those of us from the rich Western world must ask ourselves whether we are equally concerned about the poor."

[*God's Mission: Healing of the Nations*, p66] ■

BRANCH LINE
Slavery today

One of the reasons contemporary Western Christians tend to over-spiritualise the liberation story of the Exodus is that we think real slavery – the ownership of one person by another in which the victim is forced into unrewarded labour – is a thing of the past. We talk of the abolition of slavery in the same way as we talk about the demise of steam power: it was real and relevant, but isn't any more. The truth, though, is that there remains a disturbing tide of real slavery in the world today.

Slavery still exists in a number of nations:
Contemporary slavery:
- Is often associated with debt – families unable to pay their debts sell themselves, instead, into bondage.
- Predominantly involves women and children.
- Is frequently associated with the sex industry: largely financed by prosperous Western tourists.
- Can involve military service: of the 300,000 children recruited as soldiers worldwide during the 1990s, one-third were girls and many were victims of kidnap.

FREEDOM

Close Up:

A team from Jubilee Action report one desperate case of a man trying to sell his one-year-old baby into sex slavery:

'The baby's father worked as a street labourer, the poorest of the poor, in Bombay's bustling vegetable market. Tragedy struck when the girl's mother died. In turmoil, unable to cope and with intense financial pressures, the father took the child to the notorious Kamatipura, the centre of Bombay's sex industry. The man toured the brothels and offered the baby for sale. The news caused a mini sensation as the brothel owners bargained over the innocent child. The man was offered £150. But the news also reached the Jubilee team. They immediately swooped and confronted the father who seemed determined to sell the baby. After some discussion, our team convinced him not to sell the child and the father eventually handed the girl into the care of our team. The rescue was complete. The baby is safe. She has been named Glory.'

Slavery still exists as international trafficking

World Vision reports, "The commercial sexual exploitation and trafficking of children exists in every region of the world. An estimated 700,000 to one million women and children are moved across national boundaries and sold into slavery, including domestic servitude, bonded sweatshop labour and other debt bondage."

[*Every girl counts: Development, Justice and Gender*, World Vision, 2001]

This is an issue that touches the UK. We are not in the big league of slave nations, but campaigners insist that slave trafficking into the UK does exist and the UK government, acknowledging the problem, is seeking to outlaw "human trafficking for the purposes of labour or sexual exploitation."

The Exodus narrative can be read in terms of many forms of slavery; political, personal, social and spiritual. We can each find our own story within it. But it can surely also be read in terms of the real slavery that exists in the world today. If Yahweh has a word of liberation to speak to spiritual slaves, he must surely also long to free the millions held today in physical slavery. ∎

FELLOW TRAVELLERS

Wrestling or nestling?

'Paul in Ephesians 6:12 says: "For we do not wrestle against flesh and blood, but against principalities, against powers, against the rulers of the darkness of this age" (NKJ). A preacher suggested that many Christian lives could be summed up in the first five words of that text. Are you a wrestling or a resting Christian? Begin to use the power that you have been given against the forces of darkness. Don't just nestle, wrestle.'
Phillip Greenslade & Selwyn Hughes
[*Cover to Cover, God's Story*, p132]

A (Wilber)force for change

Os Guinness, in *The Call*, finds inspiration in the life of William Wilberforce, who took literally God's desire to liberate slaves – and made a decisive contribution to the framing of anti-slavery legislation in Britain.

'Wilberforce's momentous accomplishments were achieved in the face of immense odds. As regards the man himself, Wilberforce was by all accounts an ugly little man with too long a nose, a relatively weak constitution, and a despised faith – "evangelicalism" or "enthusiasm". As regards the task, the practice of slavery was almost universally accepted and the slave trade was as important to the economy of the British Empire as the defence industry is to the United Sates today. As regards his opposition, it included powerful mercantile and colonial vested interests, such national heroes as Admiral Lord Nelson, and most of the royal family. And as regards his

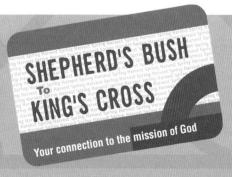

SHEPHERD'S BUSH
To
KING'S CROSS
Your connection to the mission of God

"Love breaks the chains that hold you to the past; it allows for growth, change, and new life."
Adolfo Quezada

perseverance, Wilberforce kept on tirelessly for nearly fifty years before he accomplished his goal.'
[*The Call*, p28]

Three important reminders emerge from the Exodus accounts of God's liberating actions:

Social evil is real and concrete

For those who have over-spiritualised the Exodus narrative, overlooking its social and political dimensions, it is important to be reminded of the reality of political and social oppression. There is real and concrete evil in the world, and throughout history men and women have suffered at the hands of their fellow humans. No Christian theology of evil can be complete if it ignores these concrete and visible expressions of evil in the world.

God may opposes the evil in a nation – but he does not oppose its people

It is important to remember that God's battle is not against the Egyptian people, but against the tyrannical regime of Pharaoh. In political terms, Pharaoh has violated his right to rule by actions that are unjust and inconsistent. He constantly offers freedom, only to change his mind. His own people are as much victims of his despotic obsessions as are the Hebrew slaves. It is the regime – personified in its absolute ruler – which God opposes, not the people or nation. Tony Campolo cites an ancient Hasidic story that captures this important reminder:

'The God we worship is a God who loves all people of all races and tribes. This is articulated well in a Hasidic story that tells of a great celebration in heaven after the Israelites are delivered from the Egyptians at the Red Sea, and the Egyptian armies are drowned. The angels are cheering and dancing. Everyone in heaven is full of joy. Then one of the angels asks the archangel Michael, "Where is God? Why isn't God here celebrating?" And Michael answers, "God is not here because he is off by

himself weeping. You see, many thousands of his children were drowned today!"'
[*Let Me Tell You A Story*]

True freedom is found in serving God

Terence E. Fretheim points out that the liberation spoken of in Exodus is not simply 'freedom from' but also 'freedom to'. Unless liberation leads in turn into new relationship with God, it cannot be seen as biblical freedom:

'It must be remembered that the book of Exodus insists that one cannot speak of liberation as a freeing from all restraints; it is not a declaration of independence. As we have noted, Exodus moves from one kind of slavery to another, from bondage to Pharaoh to the service of Yahweh ... Any who would use Exodus as a paradigm for liberation should move to the question, Whom will we now serve? Exodus would claim that true freedom is found only in the service of Yahweh.'
[*Interpretation: Exodus*, p20]

APPLICATION
The mopet show

Terence E. Fretheim points out that the language used in Exodus to describe the plagues is essentially the language of 'signs and wonders':

'Common parlance refers to these events as plagues (i.e. a blow or stroke), but the narrative itself uses the language of "sign" ('ot; 4:17; 7:3; 8:23; 10:1–2) and "portent (wonder)" (mopet; 4:21; 7:3; 9; 11:9–10).'
[*Interpretation: Exodus*, p107]

- How does it change your view of the Exodus story to associate it with signs and wonders?
- Does the narrative suggest a pattern in which signs and wonders play an essential part in the fulfilment of God's mission? ∎

FREEDOM

THE BOOK STALL

Andrew Walls, The Missionary Movement in Christian History: Studies in the Transmission of Faith, Edinburgh: T and T Clark, 1996

Chawkat Moucarry, Faith to Faith – Christianity and Islam in Dialogue, IVP

Chris Wright, Ambassadors to the World, IVP

Gregory Boyd, God at War, IVP

Neil T. Anderson, The Bondage Breaker, Monarch

Lesslie Newbigin, The Open Secret: An Introduction to the Theology of Mission, London: SPCK, 1995

Mark Greene, Thank God it's Monday, Scripture Union

SHEPHERD'S BUSH
To
KING'S CROSS

Your connection to the mission of God

Part Three

GOD CARES
JUSTICE & HOPE

Bible Reading, Jonah 3:1-10

¹Then the word of the LORD came to Jonah a second time: ²"Go to the great city of Nineveh and proclaim to it the message I give you."

³Jonah obeyed the word of the LORD and went to Nineveh. Now Nineveh was a very important city – a visit required three days. ⁴On the first day, Jonah started into the city. He proclaimed: "Forty more days and Nineveh will be overturned." ⁵The Ninevites believed God. They declared a fast, and all of them, from the greatest to the least, put on sackcloth.

⁶When the news reached the king of Nineveh, he rose from his throne, took off his royal robes, covered himself with sackcloth and sat down in the dust. ⁷Then he issued a proclamation in Nineveh:

"By the decree of the king and his nobles:

Do not let any man or beast, herd or flock, taste anything; do not let them eat or drink. ⁸But let man and beast be covered with sackcloth. Let everyone call urgently on God. Let them give up their evil ways and their violence. ⁹Who knows? God may yet relent and with compassion turn from his fierce anger so that we will not perish."

¹⁰When God saw what they did and how they turned from their evil ways, he had compassion and did not bring upon them the destruction he had threatened.

Overview

God cares enough about Jonah to call him a second time – and he cares enough about the people of Nineveh to send them a messenger who calls them to change.

Jonah faces a daunting task – a very large, pagan culture that was deaf to God. He sets off to do the best he can – as one tiny voice in the crowd.

But the God of surprises is at work – from marketplace to palace, the people of Nineveh respond. This is a miracle of grace.

With fasting, repentance and prayer, people seek God and his righteous judgement is stayed.

The God who cares 'had compassion' (v10) on the preacher – and on his congregation too.

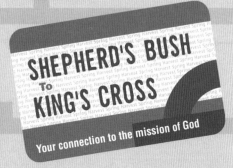

SHEPHERD'S BUSH
TO
KING'S CROSS

Your connection to the mission of God

NOTES

JUSTICE

NOTES

Exodus 5:15–6:1

[15]Then the Israelite foremen went and appealed to Pharaoh: "Why have you treated your servants this way? [16]Your servants are given no straw, yet we are told, 'Make bricks!' Your servants are being beaten, but the fault is with your own people."
[17]Pharaoh said, "Lazy, that's what you are – lazy! That is why you keep saying, 'Let us go and sacrifice to the Lord.' [18]Now get to work. You will not be given any straw, yet you must produce your full quota of bricks." ...
[6:1]Then the Lord said to Moses, "Now you will see what I will do to Pharaoh: Because of my mighty hand he will let them go; because of my mighty hand he will drive them out of his country."

Introduction

'The cab stopped ... right outside the Taj Hotel and ... people approached the open windows to try and sell us goods or to beg. One girl walked up, and looked at me.

'"Please, Uncle," she said. Uncle is a term of respect in India, used in much the same way as we would say "sir." I looked at the girl and saw that she was around ten or twelve, was very beautiful and dressed in a piece of cloth ... we moved on before I had the chance to get any money out. I turned to my friend and said how beautiful she was. "Yes," he replied, "... within a year or two she'll probably be a prostitute and then she'll be lucky to make it into her twenties."

'... later on that night ... I realised I knew who that little girl was. Her name was Jesus. One day I'll stand in front of him and hear...: "I was hungry and you did not feed me. I was thirsty and you did not give me a drink. I was a stranger and you did not invite me in, naked and you did not clothe me." And I'll say, "But when didn't I do these things?"

'He'll say, "You were in a taxi in Bombay, waiting for the traffic lights outside the Taj Hotel to change. For as much as you did not do it for the least of these, my brothers and sisters, you did not do it for me."'
David Westlake
[*Upwardly Mobile*, p44]

Throughout Christian history there has been a tension between the mercy that we receive in salvation and the obedience that God asks of us in response. We are not saved by our behaviour – but changed behaviour is demanded of us. For the Christian there can be no salva-

tion that doesn't lead to service; no conversion that is not expressed in conduct. The main biblical concept for the 'right behaviour' God asks of us is captured in the word justice, though this is often mistranslated into the English word *righteousness*.

This theme of righteousness and justice runs through the Exodus narrative like an underground river, surfacing at unexpected moments and growing as the story unfolds.

Moses begins the adventure with an untrained passion for justice and becomes the lawgiver who embodies and enacts the demands of a just God. By the end of the Exodus story, it is clear that justice has been God's agenda all along. Then, as now, a just God looks for a just people.

The liberation of the slaves from injustice and their call to live just lives become, in turn, symbols of God's hope. In the present, for every victim of wrongdoing, there is the hope that God will not forever tolerate injustice. In the future, for the whole earth, there is the hope of an age of justice and peace in the reign of God.

Without God's justice, there can be no hope. With God's justice, there is hope for all. The words later given to the prophet Jeremiah resonate with the Exodus: '"For I know the plans I have for you," declares the Lord, "plans to prosper you and not to harm you, plans to give you hope and a future."'
[Jer 29:11]

God cares – do we? ■

JUSTICE

DESTINATIONS AND DEFINITIONS
Justice

justice *noun* **1** the quality of being just; just treatment; fairness. **2** the quality of being reasonable. **3** the law, or administration of or conformity to the law • *a miscarriage of justice*. **4** (**Justice**) the title of a judge. **5** a justice of the peace. **6** *N Amer, especially US* a judge. **bring someone to justice** to arrest and try them. **do justice to someone** or **something 1** to treat them fairly or properly. **2** to show their full merit, etc. **3** *colloq* to appreciate (a meal, etc) fully. **do justice to oneself** or **do oneself justice** to fulfil one's potential. **in justice to someone** or **something** to be fair to them.
ETYMOLOGY: Anglo-Saxon as *justise*: from Latin *justitia*, from *justus* just.

© Copyright Chambers Harrap Publishers Ltd 2002

God stands against the injustice of Pharaoh's regime, and calls his liberated people to a just lifestyle. Exodus is a story of justice... ■

DISTRICT LINE

✦**Just a minute!**

Moses and the search for instant justice

Terence E. Fretheim notes three separate incidents in which Moses, before God's call has come, acts against injustice – two incidents involving Egyptian and Hebrew conflicts, and the third, in Midian, involving the harassment of Jethro's daughters by nomadic shepherds:

"The *common issue* for Moses in each of these episodes is *justice*. Three types of injustice – experienced by three types of victims and perpetrated by persons from three different peoples – are challenged:

Passage	Injustice	Victim	Oppressor
Exod 2:11	beaten (*to death*)	slave	Egyptian (*master*)
Exod 2:13	wronged	neighbour	Hebrew (*equal*)
Exod 2:17	deprivation	woman	Nomads (*male*)"

[*Interpretation: Exodus*, p44-45]

Given how little we know about Moses in his pre-Midian years, the details given of these three incidents indicate a hot pursuit of justice. Moses was a man who found it hard to let injustice lie, even when his reactions got him into trouble. This is significant in the wider context of Exodus because:

- The inclusion of these incidents in the narrative clearly indicates that this was a significant part of Moses' character – probably one that remained evident throughout his life.
- The role to which God calls Moses transforms the way he sees justice and injustice and offers him different ways of reacting – notably to let God do the fighting! But it never negates this pre-existent passion. Moses' sense of right and wrong is taken up by Yahweh, transformed for use in his service.
- A passion to know and do what is right becomes indispensable when Moses becomes not only the lawgiver for Israel, but also their first judge.

Exodus 18:13–15

In Brief:
In his earlier years, Moses is impatient for justice. He wants an immediate and decisive answer. Through years of trial and training he learns to be more patient and to trust God to establish justice. But he never loses the passion. To his dying day, he is committed to seeking right behaviour. Has God chosen Moses despite his hot pursuit of justice or because of it? The text seems to suggest that Moses' innate sense of justice and his willingness to pursue it are essential to his part in God's mission.

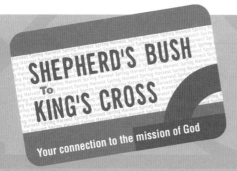

"The Hebrew words meaning justice, which unfortunately are usually translated in our English Bibles as 'righteousness', occur in various forms more than 500 times in the Old Testament. The corresponding New Testament sets of terms occur more than 200 times."
[*Thine is the Kingdom*, p52]

✦ Just not on!

Pharaoh and the offence of unjust law
When Moses brings God's message of challenge to Pharaoh, his response is to turn up the heat on the slaves, culminating in the order to make 'bricks without straw' [Exod 5:16]. The more pressure Yahweh puts on Pharaoh, the more evident the injustice of his regime becomes. Gary Haugen defines injustice in the following terms:

'Injustice occurs when power is misused to take from others what God has given to them, namely their life, dignity, liberty or the fruits of their love and labour.'
[*Good News About Injustice*, IVP, 1999, p72]

Exodus refers many times to the hardening of Pharaoh's heart. In places this is attributed to Pharaoh's own choices, in others to the sovereign hand of God. In both cases, the implication is that conflict with Yahweh will draw out more and more starkly the fundamental injustice of Pharaoh's reign. By the time the slaves reach the edge of the Red Sea, no doubt remains that this is a contest between right and wrong. God's challenges have forced Pharaoh into increasingly despotic decisions, including lies, false promises and betrayal.

In Brief:
Yahweh is not caught up in a personality clash with Pharaoh – he is fighting for justice against injustice.

✦ Just do it!

God's Law and the call for just behaviour
'Action for justice and peace in the world is not something which is secondary, marginal to the central task of evangelism. It belongs to the heart of the matter.'
Lesslie Newbigin

Finally, the outworking of the Hebrews' long walk to freedom brings them into a new phase of relationship with their God. Yahweh has not freed them simply to wander in the desert – he has a purpose and plan for them, and central to this is his justice. The Hebrew people are to be the carriers and conductors of God's justice in the world.

The justice or righteousness that God desires for his creation are embodied, for the Hebrews, in two distinct provisions. God gives them laws that carry the heartbeat of justice into every area of their lives, and he gives them judges – beginning with Moses – to help them understand and apply his law. The laws are not there to create a complex, over-legalised religious system: though for many later Jews that is what they became. They are there to reflect the character of God.

Three aspects of these laws show their great significance for the church today.
- God's laws flesh out what it means to obey: they are a response to his saving initiative
- God's laws touch on every aspect of life: there is no sacred/secular divide
- God's laws make special provision for the poor and powerless: they are about justice for all.

✦ Obedience doesn't 'win' God's approval – it expresses his character
The view that had come to dominate Judaism by the time of Jesus, that the purpose of God's Law is to provide a way of salvation, and that legal obedience is necessary for redemption, is not supported by the Exodus narrative itself. Rather, the Law describes the

"Our understanding of sin is often confined to what we call personal sins. But concern for the poor is a theme that is repeated over and over again in the Scriptures."
Ajith Fernando

JUSTICE

kind of people God wants the newborn nation to be. In the Exodus context, God's laws answer the question more recently posed by philosopher Francis Schaeffer – 'How should we then live?'

Among the pagan gods behavioural laws were always centred on appeasement: if you behaved in a certain way, the gods would not be angry with you. God's laws, by contrast, are centred on relationship: because of who God is, and because he has freed us, we will live in a way that reflects his rule.

✦ Obedience is for the whole of life

To the contemporary mind, the range and diversity of the laws given in Exodus, Leviticus and Deuteronomy strain credulity. There are temple laws, Sabbath laws, trade laws, economic laws, hygiene laws. There are laws for the behaviour of the nation and laws for the positioning of fences and the treatment of donkeys. This vast diversity arises from three aspects of the Hebrews' situation:

- They were starting with a blank piece of paper. As a slave people, the Hebrews did not have laws of their own. Their religious identity was carried by stories and family ties, and their lives were dominated by the unjust laws of Egypt; reflecting the tyranny of Pharaoh and dedicated to gods that were not Yahweh. Every area of their lives was to be re-ordered in response to God.
- They made no distinction between spiritual and secular realities. God was not the lawgiver only for the religious aspects of life – he was the lawgiver for the whole of life.
- God had called them. The power of the Exodus event was such that the Hebrews knew that they were not established by an accident of history. Yahweh who had brought them to freedom, and would define their laws and life.

The laws of God, given through Moses, responded to these conditions. They affect the whole of life: measuring up each area against the standards of God's justice.

✦ Obedience includes 'provision for the poor'

A repeated emphasis runs through the laws given to Israel: a people freed from slavery, they should never mistreat others in the ways they were once mistreated. The justice of Yahweh would be seen in the justice of his people. They would be unique: a beacon of right living in a dark world:

'God called his people Israel to be unique. He called them to be an example of social concern. They were to be committed to the poor, needy, widowed and orphaned: ruled by justice, peace and love, with no slaves or elaborate social hierarchy.'
Clive Calver
[*The Holy Spirit – Transforming Us and Our World*, p67] ■

In Brief:

Justice, then, becomes the foundation stone of the lives the people of Israel are called to lead. Their whole response to this God who has freed them can be captured in the words later used by the prophet Micah:

He has showed you, O man, what is good.
     And what does the LORD require of you?
To act justly and to love mercy
     and to walk humbly with your God.
(Mic 6:8)

Close Up:

"The Mosaic legislation showed special concern for the gerim, *the stranger or foreigner who was resident in Israel (cf. Exod 12:48; 22:21)."*
Andreas J. Köstenberger & Peter T. O'Brien
[*Salvation to the Ends of the Earth*, p35]

As strangers in Egypt, the Hebrews had been at first welcomed, but later abused. Their foreign status had been the mark by which they were set apart for slavery. Now, as a nation, they themselves would have foreigners living amongst them. Would they treat them as they had been treated – or demonstrate the unique justice of Yahweh? They had been powerless, and were oppressed by the powerful. How would they respond when the tables were turned? A just nation would not be one that simply swapped one form of oppression for another – it would be one that found a better way. The laws of God were set in place to mark out that way, and to lead Israel forward on a just path.

Main Lines

In considering the theme of biblical justice in relation to the mission of God, four key questions arise:

- **Just God:** What role does justice play in the promise-plan of God?
- **Just Jesus:** How is God's justice seen in the ministry of Jesus?
- **Just church:** How should justice be embraced in the life of the church?
- **Just world:** What are the challenges of justice in the world today? ■

JUST GOD
Justice in the plan of God

✦ Justice is an identifying mark of God's mission

'The Bible tells us that the holy, loving God we worship has a special concern for the poor, weak, and destitute. Anyone who wants to love and obey this biblical God must share the same concern.'
Ronald Sider
[*Good News and Good Works: A Theology for the Whole Gospel*]

Close Up:

"We should pause to realise," Paul Marshall suggests, "just how much of the Bible is about justice. The word *righteousness*, which we often use instead, seems to have different connotation in the modern world and is often used by Christians to mean holiness or morality. However, if we substitute, as we should, variations of the term justice wherever we read righteousness, then the Bible begins to sound quite different. We realise that justice appears and is stressed again and again throughout the Scriptures in reference to God, to Jesus Christ, to kings, judges, priests, prophets, the poor and the rich."

[*Thine is the Kingdom*, p53]

"I tell these evangelicals in the United States there are 2,300 verses of scripture about the poor. It's the central message outside of personal redemption, the idea of dealing with the poor. And I'm asking them, where are they? Where are they on this? On a recent poll of evangelical churches, only six per cent said they wanted to do something about AIDS. It is unbelievable, the leprosy of our time if you like. But it's starting to turn; the church is starting to wake up."
Bono, U2
[Interviewed by Peter Mansbridge, CBC TV's The National, Canada, June 28, 2002]

JUSTICE

The call for justice is present at every stage of the biblical narrative – and is expressed primarily in terms of concern for the weak and vulnerable. The mark of the justice of God in a community, it seems, is its treatment of the poor.

Close Up:

Clark Pinnock and Robert C Brow point out that the Old Testament Judges – the early interpreters of the law of God, who carried on the work Moses had begun in making God's justice accessible to all – were called primarily to ensure the protection of the vulnerable and the release of the oppressed: "Maybe in order to grasp the meaning of judge and judgement, we need to take a fresh look at the book of Judges, because it tells us how the Jewish people saw judges functioning. Judges were leaders empowered by the Holy Spirit to set people free from oppression. Deborah, Gideon and Samson were not law-court judges – they were leaders who took risks in order to care for people. They fought for people, led them out of bondage, and they brought peace."

[*Unbounded love*, p74]

Paul Marshall sees the same pattern, in turn, in the later period of the Kings and says "Psalm 72 ties justice in with the defence of the poor, the needy and the oppressed and, in turn, with the punishment of the oppressor." [*Thine is the Kingdom*, p51]. This psalm links the success of the king entirely to his capacity to "defend the afflicted among the people," to "save the children of the needy" and to "crush the oppressor."

Later still, the prophets consistently expressed the call for renewal in Israel's life in terms of justice, demonstrated in care for the weak.

'The prophetic voices of Scripture used the care of the poor as a touchstone by which to judge the religious establishment.'
A Church Without Walls
[Report of the Church of Scotland, p25]

In Isaiah 58 – one of the most beautiful justice passages in Scripture and an inspiration to many who work amongst the poor – the road to national revival is expressed exclusively in terms of justice: obedience to God's laws that will "loose the chains of injustice and untie the cords of the yoke, ... set the oppressed free and break every yoke" [Isa 58:6].

This emphasis, according to René Padilla, is carried over into the New Testament, where "the gospel of the kingdom is by definition 'good news to the poor'. Accordingly, the acid test of commitment to the kingdom is practical concern for the poor."
Dewi Hughes and Matthew Bennett
[*God of the Poor*, Foreword] ■

In Brief:

Expressed in terms of care for the poor and weak, justice in the Bible is presented as:
- A central aspect of God's mission in the world
- A visible sign of God's renewing presence
- An expected attribute of God's representatives and servants
- A litmus test of the obedience of God's people
- A measurable benefit of the coming of God's kingdom

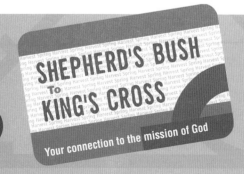

SHEPHERD'S BUSH
to
KING'S CROSS
Your connection to the mission of God

2 JUST JESUS
Justice in the ministry of Christ

✦ Justice is the heartbeat of Jesus' own sense of his calling

The ministry of Jesus continued and completed that of the Old Testament prophets, calling God's people back to the roots of their faith. In Luke 4, at the unofficial launching of his public ministry, Jesus read from the prophet Isaiah, saying:

'The Spirit of the Lord is on me,
because he has anointed me
to preach good news to the poor.
He has sent me to proclaim freedom for the prisoners
and recovery of sight for the blind,
to release the oppressed,
to proclaim the year of the Lord's favour.'

[Isa 61:1,2]

The longing of the prophet for the justice of God was "fulfilled today in your hearing," Jesus said.

[Luke 4:21]

John Stott writes: "Jesus was not afraid to look human need in the face, in all its ugly reality. And what he saw invariably moved him to compassion, and so to passionate service. Sometimes, he spoke. But his compassion never dissipated itself in words; it found expression in deeds. He saw, he felt, he acted. The movement was from the eye to the heart, and from the heart to the hand. His compassion was always aroused by the sight of need, and it always led to constructive action. It seems incontrovertible that if we are even to begin to follow the real Jesus, and to walk in his shoes, we must seize every opportunity to 'do good'. Our good works will show the genuineness of our love, and our love will show the genuineness of our faith."

[Cited in Stephen Gaukroger, *Why bother with mission?*, p62] ■

Close Up:

It has always been a feature of the life of the church, Steve Chalke claims in the *Faithworks* manual, to care for the needy and bless the poor. "…The church in Britain became the original caring profession, pioneering welfare before there even were any 'secular institutions'. In the Middle Ages it was the churches and monasteries which offered help for those who fell through the cracks in society. And when the upheavals of the eighteenth century Industrial Revolution destroyed, in just a few generations, a traditional way of life (and welfare) that had existed for hundreds of years, the church was at the forefront of attempts to stem the growing tide of poverty and outright destitution. In fact, it was only in the mid-nineteenth century that the government and statutory organisations began to think of themselves as having any significant role to play in welfare provision, and not until the second half of the twentieth century that some politicians began to think the state should have an exclusive one."

[*Faithworks: The Manual*, p14]

A prayer –
"As I expose myself to the pain of the poor, the weight of their suffering threatens to crush me. I know that I can neither carry such a weight of pain, nor do anything to lighten the burden in my own strength. I am so grateful that you are a king who has already taken all this pain to the cross and carried it away for me."
Dewi Hughes and Matthew Bennett

JUSTICE

JUST CHURCH?
Justice in the life of the church

✦**Justice is an essential ingredient in the life and calling of the church**

'The church is called by God to care for the poor, to address the causes of poverty and to learn more of Christ from being alongside the poor.'
A Church Without Walls
[Report of the Church of Scotland, p26]

Describing in Galatians 2:1 the conditions set by the Jerusalem apostles in allowing Christian churches to spread into gentile communities, Paul writes, "All they asked was that we should continue to remember the poor, the very thing I was eager to do." [Gal 2:10] Remembering the poor is a key element in the church's role in the mission of God. ■

In Brief:
Church Without Walls, the report to the Church of Scotland on cultural changes and their likely impact on the church, puts the challenge of justice in the local church like this:
'We stand accountable to the poorest people of the land. If our reshaping of the church does not give our God of love and justice a local face, then we have not touched the heart of God's covenant love.'

JUST WORLD?
The challenge of justice in the world today

✦**Justice is as needed today as it has ever been**

'We cannot be satisfied with the facile suggestion that this emphasis was only necessary in Jesus' day. Today is his moment as well. The same needs still apply. About 800 million people, one-fifth of the human race, are destitute, lacking the basic necessities for survival.'
Clive Calver
[*The Holy Spirit – Transforming Us and Our World*, p65]

The myth of human progress is that the modern and postmodern world has somehow dealt with the need for justice along the way. We refer to past peoples as barbarian and former times as the Dark Ages, and believe that our modernised and civilised world is somehow more just. The true picture, though, is more disturbing. In reality, the cry of the human heart for justice is as loud today as ever – and quite possibly louder.

"We are at a point in history," Des Summerson suggests, "when one of the greatest injustices of all time is taking place. One-third of the world lives in comparative luxury while another third lives in desperate poverty."
[*Hope in Despair*: releasing God's power to give hope to the poor and oppressed]

Jesus' parable of Lazarus and Dives – the rich man in his castle, the poor man at his gate – has proved uncannily predictive, as the world itself takes on the character of a two-tier culture. [Luke 16:19–31]

Consider some of the following expressions of the magnitude of injustice in our world:

'Communications technologies, like other economic resources, are unevenly distributed. It is a sobering fact that nine out of ten people in the world have never made a telephone call in their lives; that despite the propaganda of Bill Gates and other computer salesmen, ninety-nine out of every hundred do not have access to

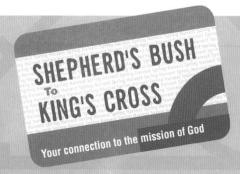

the internet; that Tokyo, with a population of 23 million, has three times as many telephone lines as the whole continent of Africa with 580 million people.'

Vinoth Ramachandra
[*Faiths in Conflict?*, p9]

- People in Europe spend more on ice cream each year than it would cost to provide clean water and sanitation for all people in developing countries.
- A child born in the industrial world adds more to consumption and pollution over his or her lifetime than 30 children born in developing countries.

United Nations
[United Nations Development Programme (UNDP) Human Development Report (HDR) cited in Dave Westlake, *Upwardly Mobile*]

- **Children:** Some 160 million children are moderately to severely malnourished.
- **Health:** Well over a billion people lack access to safe water. Nearly a third of the people in the least developed countries are not expected to survive to age 40.
- **Nutrition:** Some 840 million go hungry or face food insecurity.
- **Education:** Nearly a billion people are illiterate and 110 million children are out of school.
- **Income:** 1.3 billion people live on an income of less than the equivalent of $1 (60 pence) a day.

United Nations
[United Nations Development Programme (UNDP) Human Development Report Des Summerson, *Hope in Despair*]

'The United Nations estimates the cost of eradicating poverty at 1% of global income. Effective debt relief for the poorest countries would be even cheaper, with a price tag of $5.5billion – the cost of building Disneyland Paris.'

Victoria Brittain and Larry Elliot
[Dollar-a-day losers in the global economy, *The Guardian*, 12 June 1997, cited in Des Summerson, *Hope in Despair*]

In the face of such indicators – to which hundreds more could be added touching on war and civil war, AIDS and related health issues, pollution and environmental degradation – it is difficult not to conclude that the need for justice in our world is more acute than it has ever been. In every one of the factors cited above, the victims of poverty and injustice include an overwhelming number of children. The words of Dietrich Bonhoeffer, "The test of the morality of a society is what it does for its children," stand as a resounding indictment of human culture in the opening years of our century.

"How would history judge a generation," Pope John Paul II asked on a visit to West Africa, "which had all the means to feed the population of the planet, and yet, with fratricidal indifference, would refuse to do so?"

[Cited in Des Summerson, *Hope in Despair*]

And how will God judge a church, we might add, which knows the depth of his concern for justice, and yet does not show it? If it is true that justice is an identifying mark of the mission of God, the heartbeat of the calling of Jesus and an essential ingredient in the life of the church, then there is a need now, more than ever, for the people of God to express in words and actions the justice of the one who has set them free. ■

Branch Lines

BRANCH LINE
Justice as truth

Bryant L Myers suggests that a very close relationship exists between justice and truth. Injustice and the poverty it creates are related, he suggests, to a 'web of lies' touching both the poor and the non-poor. The poor, he says, have been deceived into accepting their lot in life. Robbed of their identity, dignity and vocation, they have been "taught to believe that they are supposed to be slaves or that it is part of the scheme of things that they should do the work of untouchables or bonded labourers. They do not believe they are intended to be creative and productive stewards."

[*Walking with the Poor*, p110]

The non-poor, meanwhile, have been deceived by different lies, persuading them to put their trust in their

"As the former archbishop of Cape Town, Desmond Tutu, observed: 'If we are to say that religion cannot be concerned with politics, then we are really saying that there is a substantial part of human life in which God's will does not run. If it is not God's, then whose is it?' The real problem our society faces isn't so much secularisation as sacralisation on the part of the church – the removal of Christian involvement, influence and truth from mainstream debate."
Steve Chalke

JUSTICE

wealth. In this sense, both Lazarus and Dives are the victims of poverty.

'The result is a life full of things and short on meaning. The non-poor simply believe in a different set of lies. At the end of the day, the poverty of the non-poor is the same kind of poverty as the poor, only differently expressed. The poverty of the non-poor is fundamentally relational and caused by sin. The only difference is that the poverty of the non-poor is harder to change.'
[*Walking with the Poor*, p90]

The truth of the gospel, in this model, is a liberating force both for the poor and for the non-poor. True freedom comes through accepting God's ways of justice and love.

"Millions of North Americans and Western Europeans are in despair as they seek in vain for happiness through ever greater material abundance," Ron Sider writes. "The idolatrous materialism of the economic rat race creates alcoholics, ruined marriages and heart attacks. Jesus, on the other hand, offers true joy – not through getting, but through giving."
[*Rich Christians in an Age of Hunger* (Revised Edition), London: Hodder and Stoughton, 1997, p xiv] ■

BRANCH LINE
Justice as a change of perspective

Part of the challenge to the people of Israel was to see the world as God sees it. In Deuteronomy 29:2–4, Moses recognises the depths of this challenge. Similarly today, the challenge to live in the justice of God, though it must in due course be expressed in action, begins with how we see things: the perspective from which we look at the world.

The *perspective* of justice can impact:

● The way we relate to God

'We long for intimacy with God, and the Bible shows us three ways of discovering it. First, we can get closer to him through our praise and worship, our prayer and relationship with him. The second is by obeying him – as he said, "those who love me will obey my commands." The third way is this: finding him in the eyes and lives of the poor.'
David Westlake
[*Upwardly Mobile*, p3]

● The way we read the Bible

'To find out the good news to the poor you must read the Bible from the underside.'
Chris Sugden
[Cited in Roger Sainsbury, *Justice on the Agenda*, p22]

● The way we approach theology

'In theologising about a "just God" we need to be involved where the injustices of society are felt.'
Roger Sainsbury
[*Justice on the Agenda*, p21]

● The way we choose *where* and *how* to live and do mission

'Jesus was himself the carrier of the message; he was at the same time the Supreme Intelligence, capable of devising the best way of making himself understood, and of carrying out the divine plans. Well, what did he do? He did not open hospitals or found orphanages. He became flesh, lived among people and he embodies the Gospel message in its entirety. .... He lived his message before he spoke of it. He preached it by his life before explaining it in words. This was Jesus' method and we too easily forget it.'
Carlo Carretto
[*Letters from the Desert*]

'There is a lot of enthusiasm about missions today, but there isn't enough teaching about the simple and eco-

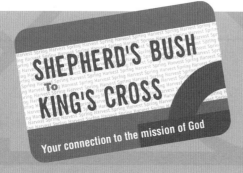
SHEPHERD'S BUSH To KING'S CROSS
Your connection to the mission of God

nomically deprived lifestyle needed to minister effectively in a world where the majority of the unreached are poor.'
Ajith Fernando
[*Spiritual Living in a Secular World*, p33]

● **The way we choose who we will befriend and spend time with**

'No amount of discussion can conceal the fact that Jesus was a partisan for the poor, the mourning, the hungry, the failure, the powerless, the insignificant. He got involved with moral failures, with obviously irreligious people: people morally and politically suspect, many dubious, obscure, hopeless types.'
Hans Kung
[Cited in Roger Sainsbury, *Justice on the Agenda*, p136] ■

BRANCH LINE
Justice as love of neighbour

The phrase that most sums up the justice of God in the Old Testament, and is loudly endorsed by Jesus in the New, is the command to "love your neighbour as yourself". John Piper suggests that this indicates not just the direction but also the measure of the love God asks of us:

'Jesus commands, "As you love yourself, so love your neighbour". Which means: As you long for food when you are hungry, so long to feed your neighbour when he is hungry. As you long for nice clothes for yourself, so long for nice clothes for your neighbour. As you desire to have a comfortable place to live, so desire a comfortable place to live for your neighbour. As you seek to be safe and secure from calamity and violence, so seek comfort and security for your neighbour. As you seek friends for yourself, so be a friend to your neighbour... The word "as" is very radical: "Love your neighbour **as** yourself". It means: if you are energetic in pursuing your own happiness, be energetic in pursuing the happiness of your neighbour. If you are creative in pursuing your own happiness, be creative in pursuing the happiness of your

neighbour. In other words Jesus is not just saying: seek for your neighbour the same things you seek for yourself, but seek them in the same way – the same zeal and energy and creativity and perseverance.'
[*Desiring God*, p282] ■

FELLOW TRAVELLERS

Kissing the Leper

Ronald Rolheiser, in *The Shattered Lantern*, re-tells a story from the life of St Francis:

'There is a story told about Francis of Assisi, perhaps more mythical than factual, which illustrates how touching the poor is the cure for a mediocre and dying faith: One night prior to his conversion, Francis, then a rich and pampered young man, donned his flashiest clothes, mounted his horse, and set off for a night of drinking and carousing. God, social justice, and the poor were not on his mind. Riding down a narrow road, he found his path blocked by a leper... Francis eventually had no other choice but to get down off his horse and try to move the leper out of his path. When he put out his hand to take the leper's arm, as he touched the leper, something inside him snapped. Suddenly irrational, unashamed, and undeterred by the smell of rotting flesh, he kissed that leper. His life was never the same again. In that kiss, Francis found the reality of God and of love in a way that would change his life forever.'

Mark Greene recounts a conversation with a taxi driver:

'A while back, I found myself in the front seat of a Mondeo mini-cab with a driver who only works for business accounts. He told me that he had had the opportunity to upgrade to a Mercedes, which would have enabled him to command higher fares. "But," he said, "I make what I need."
And it was enough.
Enough.
Now there's a novel concept.'
[*Thank God it's Monday*, p87] ■

JUSTICE

APPLICATION

The Key to Revival

Isaiah 58 suggests, in fairly direct language and with beautifully graphic images, that the pursuit of justice for the oppressed is in some mysterious way God's 'key to revival'. Read verses 1–11 and ask yourself:

- Do these words change your expectation of what revival and renewal are, and how you might seek them?
- What would be the issues highlighted in this passage if it were to your church that God had called Isaiah to deliver this message?

The Justice Prayer

Tom Wright, in *The Lord and His Prayer*, suggests that one of the ways to understand the Lord's Prayer is to see it as a cry for justice. "We live, as Jesus lived, in a world all too full of injustice, hunger, malice and evil," he writes. "This prayer cries out for justice, bread, forgiveness and deliverance. If anyone thinks those are irrelevant in today's world, let them read the newspaper and think again."

[*The Lord and His Prayer*, p2]

- How does it change your reading of the Lord's Prayer to think of it as a cry for justice and to pray it on behalf of the world's poor?

The Hitchhikers Guide to Justice

When I worked in a department store in Bristol I was living in Bath, about fifteen miles away. To save money – and because on some days I just didn't have any – I would often hitchhike home from work rather than catch the train. Usually I would walk to a spot not far from Temple Meads station, where the majority of the traffic was already likely to be heading for Bath. During the rush hour, I would be passed by thousands of cars in just a few minutes, most of them occupied by only one person. I didn't have any expectation that any of them ought to stop for me but I realised that if any of the passing drivers already knew me, they would almost certainly stop. This experience challenged my own view of poverty and need. How much would my attitudes to need change if I saw the *Big Issue* seller, the abandoned child, the hungry family or the elderly invalid as my own flesh and blood?

- How would my life change if I applied the rules I keep for friends and relatives to all those whom God brings across my path?

A Familiar Parable Re-told

A father was going away on a long trip to a distant land. He called his two sons to him and gave them each a thousand pounds. Six months later the father returned and called his older son to him. The son said, "Father, you entrusted me with one thousand pounds. Here, see, I have gained another thousand." The father replied, "Well done, my good and faithful son, I will put you in charge of many things. Come, share in your father's happiness." He then called the younger son to him. The younger son said, "Father, you entrusted me with one thousand pounds, but see, I have nothing left." "How can this be?" the father asked in dismay. "What did you do with the money?" And the younger son replied, "I lost it all to my brother, playing cards!"

Stuart Buchanan

[*On Call: Exploring God's Leading to Christian Service*, p59]

- We can accept that God would reward those who make the most of their talents, but not at the expense of others. But how much of what we call wealth and success is at the expense of others? ■

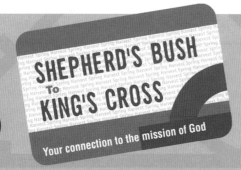

SHEPHERD'S BUSH To KING'S CROSS

Your connection to the mission of God

THE BOOK STALL

Timothy Yates, Ed., Mission: An Invitation To God's Future, Cliff College Publishing

Bryant L Myers, Walking with the Poor, Orbis Books

Steve Chalke, Faithworks: The Manual, Kingsway

Ron Sider, Rich Christians in an Age of Hunger (Revised Edition) Hodder and Stoughton, 1997

David Westlake and Craig Borlase, Upwardly Mobile, Hodder & Stoughton, 2000

Gary Haugen, Good News About Injustice, IVP, 1999

Alison Jacobs, The Road Through the Desert, Bible Reading Fellowship

Stuart Buchanan, On Call, Bible Reading Fellowship

Dewi Hughes and Matthew Bennet, God of the Poor, Authentic Lifestyle

HOPE

1 DESTINATIONS AND DEFINITIONS
Hope

hope *noun* **1** a desire for something, with some confidence or expectation of success. **2** a person, thing or event that gives one good reason for hope. **3** a reason for justifying the belief that the thing desired will still occur. **4** something desired or hoped for • *His hope is that he will pass his exams.* *verb* (**hoped, hoping**) **1** (*also* **hope for something**) to wish or desire that something may happen, especially with some reason to believe or expect that it will. **2** *intrans* to have confidence. **hope against hope** to continue hoping when all reason for it has gone; to hope in vain. **Some hope!** or **what a hope!** or **not a hope!** *colloq* there's no chance at all that what has been said will happen.
ETYMOLOGY: Anglo-Saxon *hopa*

© Copyright Chambers Harrap Publishers Ltd 2002

By his *presence* and his *promise* God calls his people to a new and different future. Exodus is a story of hope... ■

2 DISTRICT LINE
Mostar

One of the most moving worship services I have been part of took place in a former television repair shop in Mostar, Bosnia, in 1994. Around ninety people had gathered for the dedication of Viktorjia, daughter of Nikola and Sandra Skrinjaric. Nikola and Sandra had come to Mostar some twenty months earlier to reopen the city's only evangelical church, closed when the first wave of bloody conflict swept through the former Yugoslavia. The room's high windows were still stacked with sandbags and the walls outside peppered with bullet holes. The guns in the hills overlooking the city had been silenced by a cease-fire, but were not yet decommissioned, and the memories and wounds of war were fresh. Not long ago it had been impossible to enter or leave this building without ducking and diving to dodge sniper fire.

From conversations with Nikola and Sandra, I knew some of the stories of the people who gathered now to sing. There were women whose husbands, sons and brothers had been killed, or were missing. There were families whose beautiful homes, just a few miles away, were now occupied by others – taken from them by violence. Others knew that the place they had once called home was now rubble. There were children bearing the injuries of sniper fire and shrapnel wounds, others deeply traumatised by the horrors they had seen. The meeting is fixed in my memory because of one song that was used. Translated from the English, it said:

And now, let the weak say I am strong
Let the poor say I am rich
Because of what the Lord has done for me...
Give thanks.

I have sung the same song many times, and many others with it: but never in my experience has a song of worship meant so much. There were people in that gathering who had lost everything, and worse. Their whole city had been locked-down for many months: at first by daily bombardment from hillside artillery and later by house-to-house sniper fire that divided the town starkly in two.

"The lion and the calf shall lie down together: but the calf won't get much sleep."
Woody Allen

For many, their situations of poverty and loss were still unresolved: they simply didn't know what would happen to them once the war was fully over.

But they had found, in the midst of terror and heart-ache, something that had made all the difference. They had found a source of hope.

[See *Miracle in Mostar*, Gerard Kelly and Lowell Sheppard, Lion, 1995]

Close Up:

"In most ordinary speech," Lesslie Newbigin writes, "hope means little more than a desire for a better future. When I was learning to read and speak the Tamil language I slowly came to realise that it had no word for 'hope'. When I questioned my Hindu teacher about this, he asked me in turn what I meant by hope. Does hope mean anything? Things will be what they will be. I may wish that they turn out better than likely, but why should I wish to be deceived by my desires? This conversation helped me to realise that in English also the word 'hope' often stands for nothing more than a desire for what may or may not be. In contrast to this, the New Testament speaks of hope among the great enduring realities – an anchor of the soul entering in beyond the curtain which hides the future from us, something utterly reliable. ... One of the marks of the biblical counter-culture will be a confident hope that makes hopeful action possible even in situations which are, humanly speaking, hopeless. That hope is reliable, because the crucified Lord of history has risen from the dead and will come again in glory."

[*The Gospel in a Pluralist Society*, p101]

Hope is one of the foundation stones of biblical faith. Faith looks both backwards and forwards. It is founded on what God has done in the past and is doing in the present – but it is inspired by the promise of God for the future. This became the experience of the people of Israel as they walked with God beyond the immediate experience of liberation and into the future he had planned for them.

Exodus is a story of hope because:

● The promises of God are not delivered in an instant: Israel learns that there is a 'now but not yet' dimension to God's plans.
[Exodus 23:20–30]

In many senses the liberation of Israel was decisive and final: there was no going back to slavery. But in other ways, it was incomplete: it would be forty years before they would step into the Promised Land, and even then there would be battles to fight and work to be done.

The freed slaves discovered that God had placed a journey before them, with learning and discovery along the way. Even after they crossed the Jordan, without Moses, they would find, as Alison Jacobs has pointed out, that "a land of milk and honey still needs farming or the cows and bees will not produce."

[*The Road Through the Desert*, p61]

God's deliverance was decisive, but it wasn't instant. Bryant Myers writes: "It took a day to get Israel out of Egypt and forty years in the wilderness to get Egypt out of Israel."

[*Walking with the Poor*, p24]

Exodus introduces us to the now-but-not-yet dynamic of God's work: there are blessings and benefits to be received in the present, and there are others that remain future promises. Hope becomes an important dimension of God's saving acts, as we look forward to the completion of the great work that he has begun. From this point on in the biblical record, including the ministry of Jesus and the life of the early church, there is this same now-but-not-yet dimension, making hope a key characteristic of God's promise-plan.

● God assures his people that he will be with them in the walking and the waiting: a present reality to guarantee their future hope.
[Exodus 33:12–17]

"The kingdom of the broken and humiliated Christ is the only kingdom standing at the end of time."
Bryant L Myers

HOPE

In the absence of the full consummation of his promise-plan, God offers to Israel an interim blessing: the promise of his presence with them as they journey. Japanese theologian Kosuke Koyama, in *Three Mile an Hour God*, uses the walking speed of the Hebrew slaves as a measure of the speed at which God works in our lives.

"God walks 'slowly' because he is love," he writes. "If he did not love he would have gone much faster. Love has its speed. It is an inner speed. It is a spiritual speed. It is a different kind of speed from the technological speed to which we are accustomed. It goes on in the depth of our life, whether we notice or not, whether we are currently hit by storm or not, at three miles an hour. It is the speed we walk and therefore it is the speed the love of God walks."

[Cited in Tony Lane, *The Lion Concise History of Christian Thought*]

Through his presence symbolised in cloud and fire; through his extraordinary provision of food and water; through guidance; through his communion with Moses; through miraculous signs: in all these ways God let the Hebrews know that he was with them.

'In the wilderness, the Israelites had received many blessings – protection, food, water, the direct leadership of the Lord... .'
John Woolmer
[*Thinking Clearly about Prayer*, p50]

Though his promise was not instantly fulfilled, in his presence there was the assurance that it would be. The Hebrews became a people of hope because the God of hope walked with them: reminding them of all that he had done in the past and pointing them to his promise for their future.

"If God be long in coming, so be it," says the Church of Scotland report *Church Without Walls*. "If God comes quickly, we will be the more ready to welcome him and the future he brings."

It is not the *pace* of God that fills the world with hope but his *promise*: a promise guaranteed by his *presence*.

● A picture begins to emerge of greater blessings to come: the liberating God has plans for his whole creation.
[Exodus 15:11–18]

For the Hebrew slaves, the goal was the 'Promised Land'. To be set free from Pharaoh's rule; to be established in a new and free land: this was enough. But it becomes clear in the narrative that this is not the final horizon of God's plans. God's redemptive actions in liberating the slaves, Chris Wright points out, "not only provided Israel with a basis for future hope, but could be applied to the future blessing of the nations – most ironically including Egypt itself (Isa 19:19–25). ... The historic promise that God would bless the nations through Israel developed into an eschatological vision that is found particularly in Israel's worship (cf. the universal scope of Psalms 47, 87, 96) and in some of the prophets (Amos 9:12, Isa 19: 23–25, 49:6, 56:1–8, 60:1–3, 66:19–21, Zech 2:1 etc.). These texts are quite breathtaking in their universal scope. Ultimately there would be those of the nations who would not merely be joined to Israel, but would come to be identified as Israel, with the same names, privileges and responsibilities before God."
[*Christian Mission and the Old Testament: Matrix or Mismatch?*]

Hidden in the Exodus story is God's promise of redemption for his creation, sealed in the death of Jesus and promising "the time when God makes all things new, when the whole cosmos has its exodus from slavery."
Tom Wright
[*The Lord and His Prayer*, p20] ■

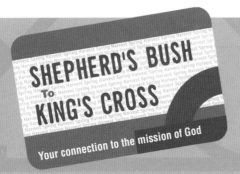

SHEPHERD'S BUSH
To
KING'S CROSS
Your connection to the mission of God

"There are no unheard prayers"
Clark Pinnock and Robert C Brow

death and resurrection (Col 2: 14–15), both Jesus and other New Testament authors see the ultimate realisation of this kingdom victory to be in the future. This constitutes the well-known 'inaugurated eschatology', or the 'already-but-not-yet' paradoxical dynamism of New Testament thought. The kingdom has already come, but it has not yet been fully manifested in world history."
[*God at War*, p213]

'So when is the kingdom coming? Simple: it has come, it is coming and it will come. It is both now and not yet. It is both imminent and immanent. This world is part of the story of God's kingdom and while the story is not complete, it is more than begun. And it is ours, both now and forever.'
Russell Rook with **Aaron White**
[*Futurize*, p22]

Main Lines

The hope of the Christian church, like that of the Hebrew slaves, follows this same three-fold pattern. Christians are people of hope because:

- They are grounded in the 'now-but-not-yet' of God's kingdom
- They have the guarantee of God's presence by his spirit
- They look to the promised day when God 'makes all things new'. ■

MAIN LINE I
Now but not yet

Christians are people of hope, firstly, because they have been called to live out the promise-plan of God. It is the clear teaching of the New Testament that this plan, described by Jesus as the kingdom of God, is intentionally given to us with a now-but-not-yet dimension.

"While Jesus proclaimed by word and deed that the kingdom had come with his arrival," Gregory Boyd writes, "and while the New Testament unequivocally proclaims that Jesus was victorious over the enemy in his ministry,

The gospel offers hope for the present, as it offers hope to overcome the darkness of the past: and it offers, supremely, hope for the future.

'... the ultimate hope that the New Testament offers is eschatological. As sure as the Lord came the first time to defeat his cosmic enemy and our oppressor in principle, just as certainly he shall return again to defeat him in fact. Because sickness, disease, war, death, sorrow and tears are not God's will, and because God is ultimately sovereign, we can have a confident assurance that someday, when his foes are ultimately vanquished, God will end all sorrow, and every evil which causes such sorrow, and will wipe away every tear from our eyes (Rev 20:4).'
Gregory Boyd
[*God at War*, p293]

It is this now-but-not-yet dynamic that defines the role of the church, as a redeemed community that walks with God, stretched between the benefits of the first coming of Christ and the promise of the second coming.

'The New Testament says that in Christ the Messiah has already come, and we have seen the kingdom. But we also look forward with longing to the Messiah's coming,

"So, hold unshakeably to the heart of our faith, which is Jesus Christ our hope – born, crucified and risen, during the time when Pontius Pilate was governor. Let nothing turn you aside from that hope."
Ignatius of Antioch

HOPE

this time his coming again. In the meantime, the church is to be the highway along which the blessing of God flows out in all directions to all the peoples of the world.'
Rose Dowsett

[*The Great Commission*, p50]

Jurgen Moltmann has argued powerfully that this emphasis on the future is the defining characteristic of biblical Christianity: "From first to last, and not merely in the epilogue, Christianity is eschatology, is hope, forward looking and forward moving, and therefore also revolutionising and transforming the present. The eschatological is not one element of Christianity, but it is the medium of Christian faith as such, the key in which everything else in it is set, the glow that suffuses everything here in the dawn of an expected new day…"

[Cited in Tony Lane, *The Lion Concise History of Christian Thought*]

If the Christian gospel is robbed of its hope for the future, it loses in the same stroke its power in the present. Past, present and future are woven together in the promise-plan of God. The certainty of God's future allows the church to fulfil its prophetic calling, bringing hope to the present reality by speaking with confidence of the coming reality of God's plans.

Merely by speaking of the promises of God for the future, the church injects new energy, new possibilities and new hope into the present.

'[For the Christian] spirituality is a matter of another reality. It is not merely a religious sentiment, a commitment, a lifestyle, let alone a political stance or a mystical-sounding buzzword. Spirituality for the follower of Christ is a matter of a different world with a different reality, different energies, different possibilities, and different prospects. The unseen, spiritual reality is not unreal. In fact it is more real – decisive over the shadow reality of the seen world.'
Os Guinness

[*The Call*, p158] ■

In Brief:

The church, Jurgen Moltmann has said, is like an arrow "sent out into the world to point to the future."

[Cited in Tony Lane, *The Lion Concise History of Christian Thought*]

MAIN LINE 2
A guaranteed inheritance

Secondly, Christians are people of hope because God is present with them, to guarantee his future promise. Hebrews 7:2 describes Jesus as "the guarantee of a better covenant" and three times, in 2 Corinthians 1:22, 2 Corinthians 5:5 and Ephesians 1:14, Paul describes the Holy Spirit as a 'deposit' guaranteeing God's future promises to us. The sense is of a down payment in terms of both quantity and quality. Like the Hebrew slaves sustained in the desert by God's presence and provision:

- We know that we can *trust* God to fulfil his promises to us, because of all that he has already done to make his presence with us possible and real.
- We know that God is *able* to fulfil his promises to us because of the evident power of his presence with us.
- We have glimpses of *how* God will fulfil his promises to us by the character and nature of his presence with us.

The coming of the Spirit at Pentecost, in this understanding, cannot be seen as an afterthought to the gospel, or simply as empowerment for service. It is, rather, the gift of God that at one and the same time both fulfils his promise to us and assures us of the promise yet to come.

SHEPHERD'S BUSH
To
KING'S CROSS
Your connection to the mission of God

"God bless mother and daddy, my brother and sister, and save the King. And oh, God, do take care of yourself, because if anything happens to you we're all sunk."
Adlai Stevenson

'The outpouring of the Spirit on all flesh is nothing less than the goal of Christ's coming, his life, his self-giving and his resurrection. ... Pentecost is not just a coda or an appendix. It is the goal of Christmas, Good Friday and Easter.'

Jurgen Moltmann

[Cited in Timothy Yates, Ed., *Mission – An Invitation To God's Future*, p29]

Andrew Lord suggests that this gift, which we understand both through God's actions in history and through his presence in our lives, is a defining factor in the mission of God, helping us to understand what God is doing, and how we can participate with him:

'Mission can be seen as the work of the Spirit to bring a foretaste of the future kingdom into the world today – the Spirit is the "first-fruits" of what is to come (Rom 8:23). ... Mission is ultimately God's, and we cannot determine how the Spirit may work, but rather we need to follow the Spirit's lead in the hope of the change our God can and will bring.'

[*Spirit, Kingdom and Mission: A Charismatic Missiology*, p11]

'Therefore we who live in the new day and rejoice in it, knowing that Jesus already reigns, yet knowing that this reign is hidden from the world, are not impatient but patient and watchful, redeeming the time and using it to set forward until its completion the work of bearing witness to that hidden reign.'

Lesslie Newbigin

[*The Gospel in a Pluralist Society*, p111] ■

MAIN LINE 3
All things made new

Lastly, Christians are people of hope because God has not been silent about his plans. God's promise for the future is not a mystery so obscure that only the enlightened can know it, nor is it a secret so guarded that only the initiated share it. God has gone public on his plans. Through the biblical record, he has left us in no doubt as to what his intentions are: He is making all things new. According to Revelation 21:4, God's last word is: 'Behold, I make all things new.'

"Mission is Christian when its gaze towards the end," Jurgen Moltmann asserts. "It looks beyond the horizon to God's new beginning: the beginning of eternal life, the beginning of the eternal kingdom, the beginning of the new earth, the beginning of the glory in which God's 'all in all' will be present. Mission is expectation of the life of the world."

[Cited in Timothy Yates, Ed., *Mission – An Invitation To God's Future*, p28]

In Brief:

Biblical scholars, as well as everyday believers, have a range of viewpoints on just what this renewed earth and heaven will contain. What is certain is that it will be a renewal – a *making new* – of God's creation. 'Behold I make all things new' is the cry of triumph of a God who has liberated his people from the grip of sin and death and has won back, by his love, the spoiled creation. 'Behold I make all things new' is the ultimate expression of the hope to which we are called. For the followers of Jesus, this is not only the future towards which we are moving; it is also the power we can know in the present. Renewal is both the journey and the destination.

"Human beings have two countries, two homelands. One is our own country, that place where each of us was born and grew up. But the other is the hidden homeland of the spirit which the eye may not see and the ear may not hear but where, by our nature, we belong."

Father Alexander Men

HOPE

Close Up:

New Testament scholar N.T. Wright finds in Revelation 21:1–5 a picture of the future a long way from popular and mis-informed notions of heaven: "Then I saw a new heaven and a new earth; for the first heaven and the first earth had passed away, and the sea was no more. And I saw the holy city, the new Jerusalem, coming down out of heaven from God, prepared as a bride adorned for her husband. And I heard a loud voice from the throne saying, 'See, the home of God is among mortals. He will dwell with them as their God; They will be his people, and God himself will be with them; He will wipe every tear from their eyes. Death will be no more; Mourning and crying and pain will be no more, for the first things have passed away.' Most Christians, if pressed, would express their future hope in terms of leaving this world and going to another one, called 'heaven'. But here, at the climatic moment of one of the greatest New Testament books, the heavenly city comes down to earth. To be sure, God's people go to heaven when they die; they pass into God's dimension of reality, and we see them no more. But Easter unveils the truth beyond the truth of mere survival, beyond the truth even of heaven; the truth that God's kingdom shall come, and his will be done, on earth as it is in heaven. Our ultimate destiny is not a disembodied heaven, just as the ultimate destiny of this created world is not to be thrown away, abandoned as secondary or shabby. It's the tyrants who want to blow the world to bits. God wants to re-create it.

'... Heaven isn't, therefore, an escapist dream, to be held out as a carrot to make people better behaved; just as God isn't an absentee landlord who looks down from a great height to see what his tenants are doing and to tell them they mustn't. Heaven is the extra dimension, the God-dimension, of all our present reality; and the God who lives there is present to us, present with us, sharing our joys and our sorrows, longing as we are longing for the day when his whole creation, heaven and earth together, will perfectly reflect his love, his wisdom, his justice, and his peace. ... God's future for his people is a newly embodied life on a renewed earth, married to a renewed heaven. This is the hope that followers of Jesus must keep before their eyes.'

[*Following Jesus: Biblical Reflections on Discipleship*, p48, 85]

'According to the Bible, the goal of humanity is bodily resurrection in the context of a new creation. The raising of Jesus of Nazareth proclaims hope for all humankind and for the whole creation.'

Clark Pinnock and Robert C Brow

[*Unbounded love*, p35]

Commenting on Romans 8:18–21, Phillip Greenslade and Selwyn Hughes suggest: "In his stunning prophetic vision, Paul sees the destiny of believers and the future of creation mysteriously intertwined. As we know, our sin dragged creation down into fallenness and frustration. Now, strangely, our redemption offers hope to a groaning world. ... Hear with wonder the promise that the power released through the new creation will one day affect the old creation. The last word in the universe will not be a groan but Joy! Joy! Joy!"

[*Cover to Cover – God's Story*, p35]

'In the end, the God who gains a victory over chaos for the sake of the world, over death for the sake of life, over injustice for the sake of shalom, is the one for whom we desperately and unwittingly yearn. This is not an ecclesial matter, and evangelism is not in the end an ecclesial agenda. It is rather an offer that we might be on the receiving end of all things new.'

Walter Brueggemann

[*Biblical Perspectives on Evangelism*, p130] ∎

Branch Lines

BRANCH LINE
Desert roads

One of the lessons of the now-but-not-yet experience of the Hebrew slaves in their wilderness years is that God is with us on the desert road. There are times in human experience when we sense we are passing through a desert landscape.

Alison Jacobs says of this desert road that it is not "about 'wilderness spirituality' – voluntary withdrawal into an empty place in order to meet God. It is about what you might call 'exile spirituality', about finding yourself somewhere you do not want to be and looking for God in that situation. It is about wilderness as prison rather than as liberation – yet strangely enough, liberation may still be found there."

[*The Road Through the Desert: Making Sense of Wilderness Times*, p6]

Close Up:

Margaret Silf, in *Sacred Spaces: Stations on a Celtic Way*, uses an image from the novel *Away*, by Jane Urquhart. "Urquhart enters into the lives of Irish immigrants struggling in nineteenth-century Canada to wrest a living from the unyielding landscape of the Canadian Shield," she writes. "For years they live in the extreme poverty of subsistence farming that barely keeps them alive. 'How's a man supposed to farm,' one of them asks, 'when under everything there's all this rock?' We might ask the same question sometimes of our own lives' landscape. Our poverty may not be material, but emotional or spiritual. Our empty barren places may be in the aching depths of our longings and our deepest disappointments. How are we supposed to live full lives, we might ask ourselves, with all this hard rock of pain underneath?"

A victim of ME over a number of years, Jacobs has written movingly of finding the presence and purpose of God in times a great confusion and frustration – times when it seems that the very landscape of our lives is against us.

'Exile' is an aspect of spirituality all too often forgotten in a culture fixed on success. The desert places in our lives are not always places we have chosen for their beauty and solitude. Sometimes they are places forced upon us. We may have looked for – and perhaps seen – a great victory from God, but we are then faced with the day-to-day grind of walking through a barren and hard place. For all God's greatness at the Red Sea, the grind of the desert made the Hebrews long for slavery again. What does the patience, provision, protection and presence of God for the Hebrew slaves in their wilderness tell us about what we should look for in ours?

Close Up:

It is significant that for Moses this was not the first experience of wilderness years. God had used a time of exile in the harsh mountains of Midian as preparation for his leadership role – so much so that Moses named his first son Gershom, a name that sounds in Hebrew like 'an alien there', saying 'I have become an alien in a foreign land' [Exod 2:22]. Moses knew both the costs and the benefits of 'desert times'.

'In this place of solitude and holiness Moses' life was transformed, and he became the man to lead the people of God out of slavery into freedom. It could have been said that Moses' flight from the Egyptian court was a fleeing from his social and political responsibilities, a retreat into the wilderness of irrelevance and selfish piety. But that's where the presence was, and that's where the action was! God's ways are not our ways.'
Brother Ramon
[*Deeper Into God: A Handbook on Spiritual Retreats*, p25]

"If God can do more than we ask or imagine, why not ask for more imagination?"
Dave Davidson

HOPE

Viv Thomas, in *Second Choice: embracing life as it is*, argues from the life of Daniel that God does not always give us our 'first choice' lifestyle. Sometimes we must make do with a second choice – and Christian maturity is to be found in coming to terms with the reality in which God has placed us. Thomas quotes the late Henri Nouwen: "Somehow, in the midst of our tears, a gift is hidden. Somehow, in the midst of our mourning, the first steps of the dance take place. Somehow, the cries that well up from our losses belong to our song of gratitude."

[*Second Choice: embracing life as it is*, p12]

"I keep looking, God, for the dramatic moment when I can engage in a glorious sacrifice for the faith," Eugene Peterson writes. "You keep presenting me with daily opportunities for belief and obedience and hope. Help me to forget my dreams of melodrama, and accept the reality of your kingdom."

[Cited in Russell Rook and Aaron White, *Futurize*, p89] ■

In Brief:
In the now-but-not-yet of God's promises, we will face passages on our journey that do not speak to us of success and victory, but rather of hardship and adversity. Is our grasp of the hope of God strong enough, in such times, to sustain us? Will we press on in the journey, despite the hardness of the terrain?

BRANCH LINE
Hope today

Christian hope becomes a vital dimension of mission when it meets with a culture with a poor vision of the future and no substantial source of personal or social hope. Robert Warren suggests that this is the case in the postmodern West: "Today's culture is particularly in need of beginning at the end," he writes, "for we live without hope, direction or purpose."

[Cited in Andrew Lord, *Spirit, Kingdom and Mission: A Charismatic Missiology*, p9]

The proclamation of Christ in such a context, Lesslie Newbigin suggests, offers people the possibility of understanding what God is doing in history, and of recovering purpose, direction and vocation. They can begin to receive "a vision of the goal of human history ... a vision which makes it possible to act hopefully when there is no earthly hope, to find a way when everything is dark and there are no earthly landmarks."

[Cited in Bryant L Myers, *Walking with the Poor*, p204]

Clark Pinnock and Robert C Brow put the challenge to the church in stark and simple terms: "People who hope do more for this world than those without hope."

[*Unbounded love*, p41] ■

In Brief:
The recovery of Christian hope is not simply a question of finding consolation for believers who are passing through desert times – though this is a significant part of its job. Much more widely, it is about recovering an essential part of the gospel message, a vital ingredient in the mission of the church: to offer hope to a world that has none. The promise-plan of God; the future he holds for us; the now-but-not-yet of his kingdom – all these are good news indeed to those who are "without hope and without God in the world." [Eph 2:12]

BRANCH LINE
The language of hope is prayer

If Israel learned nothing else in the wilderness, they learned how to pray. It is the now-but-not-yet of God's plan, that teaches us the meaning of prayer. We learn as much during God's delays as we do in his deliveries. This in-between time, when we know God's promises but do not see their fulfilment, is the very time that will teach us the meaning of prayer. Prayer is the language of hope.

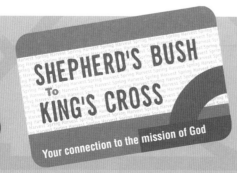

SHEPHERD'S BUSH
To
KING'S CROSS
Your connection to the mission of God

"The heart of reform is the reform of the heart," the Church of Scotland report *A Church Without Walls* says. "People at prayer will be people who learn to live within the purposes of God with patient hope."

[*A Church Without Walls*, p37]

"Prayer is a walkie-talkie for warfare, not a domestic intercom for increasing our convenience," John Piper writes. "The point of prayer is empowering for mission."

[*Desiring God*, p152]

"The best style of prayer," Charles Spurgeon wrote, "is that which cannot be called anything else but a cry."

[Cited in Ajith Fernando, *Spiritual Living in a Secular World*, p139]

The desperation of prayer that is shaped more by conflict than by comfort, more by opposition than by ease, is captured in an early Celtic prayer recorded by Bede in *The life of Cuthbert*: "The land is bleak with snow, clouds lour in the sky, there is a gale raging and the sea is a fury of waves, we are dying of hunger and there is no chance of human aid. Then let us storm heaven with our prayers, asking that the same Lord who parted the Red Sea and fed his people in the desert take pity on us in our peril."

[Cited in Michael Mitton, *Restoring the Woven Cord*, p129] ■

 ## FELLOW TRAVELLERS

Hope in Desperate Places

'At the height of the civil war in Bosnia I went there on behalf of Christian Aid to see if we could work together with some of the Islamic relief organisations in delivering relief to all those in need and not just to those of our confession. At one point we were taken to Nagorny Vaquf, a town at the centre of some of the most horrible massacres during that particularly bloody conflict. I was shown the road that divided the communities and was told how the Muslims knew very well the Serbs who had killed their relatives, and vice versa. Even indirect negotiations seemed very distant and yet, in the middle of that extremely tense and violent situation, there was

a small Christian community working for reconciliation! One could not find a more unpromising mission field (and, believe me, I have seen a few) but the Easter faith makes the Easter people do some strange things. The San Egidio community, based in Rome, but working all over the world, were able to broker a peace in another civil war – that in Mozambique – because, according to their own testimony, they were the only group who had no arms, no power and no money. This is one of the reasons why they were trusted on all sides. There is still a lot to say for the powerlessness of the Christian missionary.'
Michael Nazir-Ali

[*Shapes of Church to Come*, p38]

Prayer in Dark Places

Jenny Robertson quotes a letter of Anatoly Emmanuilovich Levitin, a Russian Orthodox believer who even in old age was harassed by the KGB and twice imprisoned for his faith. Writing from prison, the elderly saint said:

'The greatest miracle of all is prayer. I have only to turn my thoughts to God and I suddenly feel a strength which bursts into me from somewhere, bursts into my soul, into my entire being. What is it? Psychotherapy? No, it is not psychotherapy, for where would I, an insignificant, tired old man, get this strength which renews me and saves me, lifting me above the earth? It comes from without and there is no force on earth that can even understand it.'

[*Windows to Eternity*, p28] ■

 ## APPLICATIONS

A Prayer for the Desert Places

'My Lord God, I have no idea where I am going. I do not see the road ahead of me. I cannot know for certain where it will end. Nor do I really know myself, and the fact that I think I am following your will does not mean that I am actually doing so. But I believe that the desire to please you does in fact please you. And I hope I have that desire for all that I am doing. I hope that

HOPE

I will never do anything apart from that desire. And I know that if I do this you will lead me by the right road, though I may know nothing about it.

'Therefore I will trust you always though I may seem to be lost and in the shadow of death. I will not fear, for you are ever with me, and you will never leave me to face my perils alone.'

Thomas Merton

[Cited in John Moses, *The Desert*, p69]

- Does this kind of prayer speak to you of a lack of faith, or of a realistic hope?
- What do you do in your own spiritual walk to find hope in desert places? ■

CONNECTIONS
How to be Good by Nick Hornby (Viking, 2001)

Summary

Being Good and Seeking Justice

Katie knows what being good is: "I wanted to become a doctor because I thought it would be a good – as in Good, rather than exciting or well-paid or glamorous – thing to do." (p6) Her angry and irritating husband, David, visits the mysteri-

ous healer DJ GoodNews and returns with his cynicism erased. David is determined to improve the world – he begins solving the homelessness problem and starts to write a book called *How to be Good*. As far as Katie is concerned, all David's good deeds just make her look bad.

Meanwhile, their marriage is floundering and the children, Tom and Molly, are bewildered by the new regime.

Molly sides with David, while Tom and Katie unite in resisting David's irrefutable logic as he gives away their possessions and Sunday lunch. As David's efforts and enthusiasm finally falter, Katie concludes that if she can just keep the family going, that will be good enough.

So what does it mean to be good? How do we seek justice on a personal and local level? Does it mean caring for the homeless and living for social action? What does the Bible say about being good? ■

Bible Study

1 Doing good

The word 'charity' reels me back in. 'Charity vaunteth not itself, is not puffed up,' the man with the puff says. Hurrah for St Paul! Right on! Vaunting and puffing! Puffing and vaunting! You want any of that, you should come round to Webster Road, which has become a Puffers and Vaunters Social Club! Why had I never heard this stuff properly before? (Katie, p189)

- Read Matthew 6:1–4. Why, according to Jesus, do some people do good things in public? What does Jesus recommend instead?
- Read 1 Corinthians 13. What might someone be hoping to gain through the actions described in verses 1–3? Why don't they count without love?

2 Made good

It's not enough to be a doctor, you have to be a good doctor, you have to be nice to people, you have to be conscientious and dedicated and wise, and though I enter the surgery each morning with the determination to be exactly those things, it only takes a couple of my favourite patients – a Barmy Brian, say, or one of the sixty-a-day smokers who are aggressive about my failure to deal with their chest complaints – and I'm ill-tempered, sarcastic, bored. (Katie, p179)

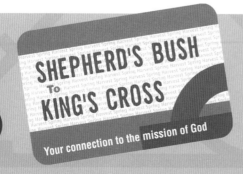

SHEPHERD'S BUSH
TO
KING'S CROSS

Your connection to the mission of God

- Read 2 Peter 1:1–11. How does Peter say we should be good? What is the balance between what God does and what we do?
- Read Romans 3:9–31. What does Paul say about our attempts to be good? How does God make us good? What responsibilities does this leave us with?

Implications

Who are these people, that they want to save the world and yet they are incapable of forming proper relationships with anybody? As GoodNews so eloquently puts it, it's love this and love that, but of course it's so easy to love someone you don't know, whether it's George Clooney or Monkey. Staying civil to someone with whom you've ever shared Christmas turkey – now there's a miracle. (Katie, p220)

- How do you feel about social action? Are you motivated to change your world? Why? What would you say to Katie and David about their attempts to be good?
- Why doesn't going to church make you good? What would you say to a friend who thinks they are not good enough to go to church?

From *Connect Bible Studies: What does the Bible say about... How to be Good*. ISBN 1 85999 610 8 published online by Damaris, and in print by Scripture Union – Linking the Word to the World. www.connectbiblestudies.com – these studies are available to buy from this site. ■

THE BOOK STALL

Tom Wright, Following Jesus – Biblical Reflections on Discipleship, London: SPCK, 1998

Ajith Fernando, Spiritual Living in a Secular World, Monarch

Russell Rook and Aaron White, Futurise, Spring Harvest / Authentic, 2002

Part Four

GOD RULES

WORSHIP & COMMUNITY

Bible Reading, Jonah 4:1-11

¹But Jonah was greatly displeased and became angry. ²He prayed to the LORD, "O LORD, is this not what I said when I was still at home? That is why I was so quick to flee to Tarshish. I knew that you are a gracious and compassionate God, slow to anger and abounding in love, a God who relents from sending calamity. ³Now, O LORD, take away my life, for it is better for me to die than to live."

⁴But the LORD replied, "Have you any right to be angry?"

⁵Jonah went out and sat down at a place east of the city. There he made himself a shelter, sat in its shade and waited to see what would happen to the city. ⁶Then the LORD God provided a vine and made it grow up over Jonah to give shade for his head to ease his discomfort, and Jonah was very happy about the vine. ⁷But at dawn the next day God provided a worm, which chewed the vine so that it withered. ⁸When the sun rose, God provided a scorching east wind, and the sun blazed on Jonah's head so that he grew faint. He wanted to die, and said, "It would be better for me to die than to live."

⁹But God said to Jonah, "Do you have a right to be angry about the vine?"

"I do," he said. "I am angry enough to die."

¹⁰But the LORD said, "You have been concerned about this vine, though you did not tend it or make it grow. It sprang up overnight and died overnight. ¹¹But Nineveh has more than a hundred and twenty thousand people who cannot tell their right hand from their left, and many cattle as well. Should I not be concerned about that great city?"

Overview

Jonah has a major sulk – because God doesn't fit his framework. He forgets he has received mercy and can't understand why others should also be kissed by grace.

His inconsistency is exposed when he tells God he wants to die. Here is a prophet of the Lord who is totally fed up with the Mission of God.

God takes Jonah on a nature walk and teaches him an unforgettable lesson about the heart of the Lord of heaven and earth. Why is Jonah more upset about a dead plant than dying people?

Here is our great missionary God.

And we are left with a burning challenge; whose agenda rules my life – mine – or God's?

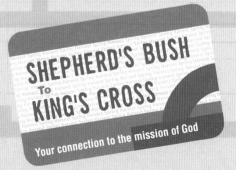

SHEPHERD'S BUSH
TO
KING'S CROSS
Your connection to the mission of God

NOTES

WORSHIP

Worship & Community:

'You belong to me' Ex 3:12 , 19:3-6 , 15:1-21.

Worship & mission belong together.

How do we worship: in silence , listening to God , read hymns , words of scripture,

enjoying creation , adoring God (use ABC of God's characteristics) ,

loving your enemy , in good relationships with others , working in kitchen

power of praise (praise) (tapes if atmosphere tense) , { through service cleaning loose etc at church

[Holy living is doing God's service with a smile]

candle , creative arts (dance, art...)

At home
Encourage e.o. to find ways to worship Him that are appropriate to them.

Mission of God is tied into worship of God.

Worship in our households — music.

1 Pet 2:4-12

• a radical change of allegiance v 9, 10.

'out of darkness into his wonderful light'.

• a radical change of community vv 4-9

many people feel isolation, we though belong to 1 father (stones in same building / Priests in same temple / citizens in same nation)

• a radical change of conduct v 11, 12.

privileges of being in God's family → responsibility to declare God's praises in conduct.

Live such attractive/beautiful lives . (see p 119)

> **Exodus 6:6–8**
>
> ⁶"Therefore, say to the Israelites: 'I am the LORD, and I will bring you out from under the yoke of the Egyptians. I will free you from being slaves to them, and I will redeem you with an outstretched arm and with mighty acts of judgment. ⁷I will take you as my own people, and I will be your God. Then you will know that I am the LORD your God, who brought you out from under the yoke of the Egyptians. ⁸And I will bring you to the land I swore with uplifted hand to give to Abraham, to Isaac and to Jacob. I will give it to you as a possession. I am the LORD.'"

Introduction

In the 1997 blockbuster *Ransom*, Mel Gibson plays the part of an airline tycoon. Starting from nothing, he has built a global business empire and now has everything. But when his only son is kidnapped, he seems to have lost it all. Wealth means nothing beside the loss of his son. He becomes totally focussed on tracking down the kidnappers and securing his son's release. In one of the film's most dramatic moments, overwhelmed by passion, he screams down a phone line to the kidnappers, "Give me back my son!"

Rewind thirty centuries or so, to a rocky hillside in Midian. God has spoken to Moses about freeing the people of Israel from slavery. Moses is to go to Pharaoh – the world's most powerful leader, head of the adopted family Moses has not communicated with in forty years – and insist that he release the Hebrews from their oppressive labour so that they can travel into the desert to worship their God. As Moses heads back with his family towards Egypt, God reminds him of what he is to say to Pharaoh.

Then say to Pharaoh, 'This is what the LORD says: Israel is my firstborn son, and I told you, "Let my son go, so that he may worship me."'
[Exod 4:22]

With these words God reveals to Moses – and to Pharaoh – the purpose of his saving initiative. It is the fatherhood of God that is at issue, and worship is the goal he has in mind. A little later, God gives Moses a promise to pass on to the weary slaves: "I will take you as my own people, and I will be your God."
[Exod 6:7]

'These two promises will serve as two parts of the tripartite formula to be repeated in the Old and New Testaments almost fifty times: "I will be your God, you shall be my people and I will dwell in the midst of you"

(cf. Gen 17:7–8; 28:21; Exod 29:45–46; Lev 11:45 et al.)'
[*Expository Bible Commentary*]

The slaves are not set free purely for the sake of freedom but to worship and become the people of God. Throughout the Exodus narrative, God is at work:

- To call a people to himself – building a community that reflects his care and character: a God-tribe that carries the family likeness. The freed slaves are to be the first fruits of the liberating reign of God – a community of the redeemed.
- To bring that people into the freedom and joy of worship – God wants his people to know the highest pleasure that it is possible to know, and the highest pleasure is his pleasure. The worship of Yahweh will so shape their lives and thinking that they begin to reflect once more his image.

At the very beginning of the world, when God had shaped a garden and called a woman and a man to care for it, we are told that the Lord God 'walked in the garden, in the cool of the day' [Gen 3:8]. The earth itself was a crucible of intimacy: a place of relaxed communion for the Creator and his creatures. Now, in a world a million miles from that ideal, God seeks out those who will worship 'in spirit and truth' [John 4:23]. Recreating contact; renewing relationship; returning to a lost intimacy – these have always been the goals of the Father who loves us. God has always been looking for a people who will worship him. Worship and community are the twin goals of a Father in search of his lost children.

God rules – do we respond? ■

WORSHIP

DESTINATIONS AND DEFINITIONS
Worship

worship *verb* (**worshipped**, **worshipping**) **1** *tr & intr* to honour (God or a god) with praise, prayer, hymns, etc. **2** to love or admire someone or something, especially blindly; to idolise them or it. **3** to glorify or exalt (material things, eg money). *noun* **1 a** the activity of worshipping; **b** the worship itself. **2** a religious service in which God or a god is honoured • *morning worship*. **3** the title used to address or refer to a mayor or magistrate, usually in the form of **His** or **Her Worship** or **Your Worship**. **worshipper** *noun*.

ETYMOLOGY: Anglo-Saxon *weorthscipe*, meaning 'worthship'.

© Copyright Chambers Harrap Publishers Ltd 2002

God does not set his people free to wander but to worship. He calls them to himself – to know him, to love him and to honour his name in all the earth. Exodus is a story of worship... ■

District Lines

The 'thread of worship' of the Exodus narrative is expressed in three key transitions that take place. God moves his people:

- **From slavery to song –**
  The freedom of the children of Israel has a purpose. They are released into worship. Worshippers give thanks for the freedom that is theirs in the victory of God.
- **From servitude to servanthood –**
  An unwanted bondage to a harsh and unjust master is replaced by a voluntary bonding to a loving God. Worshippers acclaim the rule of God over their lives and over the earth.
- **From solitude to sanctuary –**
  A people who feared that their God has forgotten them receive the promise of his presence with them. Worshippers dare to declare that God dwells among his people. ■

FROM SLAVERY TO SONG
Worship is freedom

Exodus 3:12

From the beginning God makes clear to Moses the connection between freedom and worship. The worship of Yahweh will be a sign to Moses, because only a free people can worship. The slavery of the Hebrews is not slavery to Pharaoh alone – it is also slavery to his gods. The labour of the slaves' hands is being misdirected towards the goals of a false religion – enabling Pharaoh to build the structures that will show the world how great the gods of Egypt are. "But when I set you free," God promises Moses, "this is how free you will be – you will be free to worship me." In your freedom, you will worship, and by your worship you will know that you are free. Worship is both the meaning and the measure of freedom.

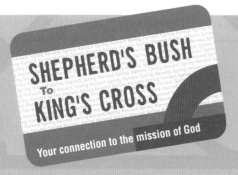

"One of the marvellous truths about the one true God who has been revealed to us through Jesus is this: he is totally and utterly worthy of our worship. He doesn't just invite or demand it, he is worth it, with a worthiness that will absorb our wondering minds for eternity."
Graham Kendrick

n Brief:
he new-found freedom of the Hebrew slaves enables
hem to worship God – and tells them exactly where
vorship begins: "True praise is a thankful, joyful, re-
cital of God's character and saving deeds. And nobody
sings about this God more than freed slaves."

Phillip Greenslade and ***Selwyn Hughes***
[*Cover to Cover – God's Story*, p133]

FROM SERVITUDE TO SERVANTHOOD
Worship is allegiance

Exodus 5:15–16

Leviticus 25:55

Deuteronomy 10:12

Joshua 24:14–15

The people who begin this adventure as the slaves of
Pharaoh end it as servants of God. The alternative to
servitude to the false gods of Egypt and Canaan is not
religious neutrality but joyful submission to the one
God, Yahweh: the Creator who has revealed himself as
Redeemer.

As the slaves are set free, they discover that God is
offering an alternative contract. If they agree to put
him first, and to allow their lives – personally, corporately and nationally – to be shaped by the centrality
of worship, they will become in reality the servants of
God in the earth. Their worship has a part to play in
the promise-plan of God – the attitude of their hearts is
central to his purposes. ■

themselves ...
[*Interpretation: Exodus*, p263]

"In the final analysis," Mark Stibbe says, "the cry of the
Father is this: 'Let my people go that they may worship
me.' God's great desire is for his people to be set free
from all forms of slavery so that they may enjoy intimacy
with him in worship."
[*From Orphans to Heirs*, p44] ■

Close Up:
On at least two occasions Moses publicly leads the
people of Israel in songs that celebrate God's victory
[Exod 15:1–18, Deut 31:30–43].

*"People say that we must have quiet,
proper, decorous services. I say,
where is your authority for this?!"*
Catherine Booth

WORSHIP

Close Up:

Servanthood bridges the gap between worship and obedience. It begins with attitude and leads to action. It is belief manifested in behaviour. This godly partnership runs through the laws that are given to Israel. Obedience without worship is not demanded: the foundation of obedience is the acknowledgement of God's character and kindness. But neither is worship without obedience countenanced. Rather, a life of worship will issue in obedience. The people will serve God in their worship, and serve God in their lives.

In Brief:

For Israel, it is worship that will give motivation and meaning to obedience. The cycle of public worship will bring the people back, time and again, to who God is, to what God has done and to what God asks of them.

FROM SOLITUDE TO SANCTUARY
Worship is presence

Exodus 25:8–9

'Nearly one-third of the book of Exodus is devoted to considerations regarding the tabernacle, Israel's wilderness sanctuary.'
Terence E. Fretheim
[*Interpretation: Exodus*, p263]

Chapters 25 to 31 are taken up with the detailed, complex instructions for the completion of this 'movable feast' of worship, a 'mobile home for God'.

In the big picture, the tabernacle establishes three key principles for the worship of the people of Israel.

The tabernacle places worship as the very heart and hub of the travelling community

For the wandering tribes of Israel the tabernacle puts worship "at the centre of their lives. The many months at Sinai are given to the structuring of a magnificent mobile worship centre: the Tabernacle. It is not a great hall for the assembling of multitudes, but a place of personal encounter where worshippers may bring their covenant offerings."
Jack Hayford
[*Worship his Majesty*, p79]

This is a revolution in the history of worship; it could never be the same once the claims of Yahweh were admitted.

'To say there is one God and no god is not simply an article in a creed. It is an overpowering, brain-hammering, heart-stopping truth that is a command to love the only one worthy of our entire and unswerving allegiance.'
Os Guinness
[Cited in Rosemary Dowsett, *The Great Commission*, p44]

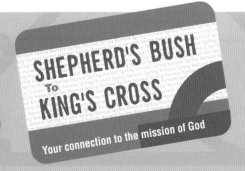

SHEPHERD'S BUSH
To
KING'S CROSS
Your connection to the mission of God

"The divine dance of Father Son and Holy Spirit draws us into their energising and invigorating movement. In our worship and in our mission we are participating in the intimate life of God."
Pete Ward

Close Up:

Three revolutionary changes are introduced by the tabernacle passages:

● The pagan gods were many, like planets of different sizes moving through the universe. Yahweh would be the one and only God, burning like the sun at the heart of all else.

● Among the pagans, the gods were part of life but not the heart of life. Yahweh, by contrast, would be the single, fixed hub of all things.

● Pagan worship was geographically defined. Gods had their turf, and worshippers would travel to their shrines and altars, the high places and holy places at which their power was known. Yahweh would be a God of no fixed abode, moving with his people as they journeyed. The God of the whole earth, his territory had neither boundary nor end.

The people of Israel, as they crossed the desert and ultimately entered Canaan, would pass through the territory of many different gods. Their instinct as slaves would be to pay their respects in passing. But God would have none of this. Rather than see his people pushed like a pinball from one god to another, he himself would journey with them. Their community would be centred on him.

In Brief:

The worship of Yahweh would be the core around which the life of Israel revolved. Worship would not just be a part of their lives; one activity amongst many. It would be the heart of their lives: the defining reality from which all else flowed.

The tabernacle creates a space in which the presence of God can be embraced and enjoyed

'The tabernacle was very costly in time, effort, and monetary value; yet in its significance and function it pointed to the chief end of man: to glorify God and to enjoy him forever. Above every other consideration was the fact that the omnipotent, unchanging, and transcendent God of all the universe had, by means of the tabernacle, graciously come to 'dwell' or 'tabernacle' with his people... .'
[Expository Bible Commentary]

The defining characteristic of the people of Israel was that God was with them. Their strength, their identity and their purpose all came from this one fact: and the tabernacle was the vehicle by which the Lord would make his presence known.

In Brief:

For Israel, worship was more than words. It was not a symbolic exploration of the idea of God's presence, but a celebration of the reality of his presence. God dwelt among his people. His presence was as real as that of Moses.

In the tabernacle, the reign of God over all the earth is acknowledged, anticipated and enacted

The creational language of Exodus presents the tabernacle as a microcosm of the wider creation. Here the desire of God to indwell his creation is received rather than resisted: expressed rather than excluded. God is doing battle on behalf of the life of his creation, re-establishing the intimacy of Eden: and though it will take time before his glory fills the earth once more; here in the tabernacle, a start has been made. Here the first fruits of the reign of God are enjoyed. Here the promise of his ultimate reign becomes a song.

"Worship is the crucible where real life and experience meet theology head on."
Maggi Dawn

WORSHIP

Yahweh is the king of all creation and here – even if nowhere else – his subjects will pay homage. Joshua's phrase 'as for me and my house' [Josh 24:15] represents a challenge faced by every child of Israel. Even if the whole world rejects the reign of God; even when rebellions break out on every side; even though no one else in all the earth may pay him due: still we will praise him. ■

MAIN LINE
Worship and the mission of God

All too often in the church, worship and mission have been seen as separate activities; distinct and unconnected. We keep worship in one compartment of our lives: broadly associated with the programmes of our churches and relating, very often, to our personal well being and fulfilment. We place the mission of God elsewhere: in a compartment that relates to action, to those outside the church, and to the work of professional missionaries.

But the biblical view of mission and worship will not allow this. In Exodus, as elsewhere in Scripture, we are introduced to a vision of worship that is intertwined with mission, and of mission that is interlaced with worship. The mission of God is tied-in to the worship of God: so closely that at times the two are one. Four key stages can be identified in the 'dance' between God's mission and our worship:

- Worship explores mission. The mission of God provides the content and context to which our worship is a grateful response.

- Mission enhances worship. The things we explore and celebrate in our worship drive us to find our own place in the plans of God, adding purpose to our praise.

Worship without mission lacks purpose.
Mission w worship lacks power.

'I've been challenged on this a lot recently. I say I'm a worship leader, and I also say that worship is far more than just about music. So why are all my acts of worship leading done through music? When it comes to reaching the broken of this world, why am I so often near the back of the queue? I'm longing to be a worshipper who sets an example for others to follow, not just with my

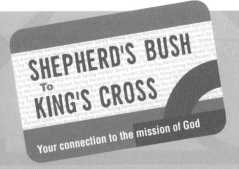

SHEPHERD'S BUSH
TO
KING'S CROSS
Your connection to the mission of God

In Brief:

As we worship God in spirit and truth, we are motivated to join with him in his purposes for the world. We feel drawn to participate in God's mission. And as we participate, it is in worship that we are equipped and commissioned for the roles to which we are called. Worship without mission lacks purpose: mission without worship lacks power.

lips, but with my life. God has made it very clear that worship and justice are inseparable.'
Matt Redman

[*The Unquenchable Worshipper*]

'It could be summed up in the statement: to worship is to be changed. ... If we are changed by getting to know people, how much more profound must be the changes brought about by getting to know God?'
Graham Kendrick

[*Worship*, p174]

● <u>**Worship energises mission.**</u> **Mission without worship is like a car with no fuel. Worship is the fission that fuels the heart of mission.**

In Brief:

It is through worship that we find the strength and inspiration we need for the tasks and trials to which God has called us. It is in worship that we are renewed, to 'soar on with wings like eagles.'

[Isa 40:31]

'Unless he is at the centre of all that we do, with actions flowing out of our relationship with him, we might as well shut up our churches and go and join the secular caring agency down the road.'
Fran Beckett

[*Called To Action*, p68]

'I tell our staff that Christian ministers are people who get their strength from God, go into the world and get bashed around. Then we come back, get our strength from God, go back into the world, get bashed around. And that is our life. We go, get bashed, get strength, go, get bashed, get strength. And we can take on strength in this way.'
Ajith Fernando

[*Missionaries for the Right Reasons*, 1997]

● **Mission extends worship. Worship is the goal towards which God's mission is moving. The future of mission is God's glory covering the earth like an ocean.**

In Brief:

The future towards which the promise-plan of God is moving can be summed up in one simple phrase: the world will worship Jesus. Worship is the final goal and objective of all mission. Where mission is effective, worship is the fruit.

'Mission is not the ultimate goal of the church. Worship is. Missions exist because worship doesn't. Worship is ultimate, not missions, because God is ultimate, not man. When this age is over, and the countless millions of the redeemed fall on their faces before the throne of God, missions will be no more. It is a temporary necessity. But worship abides forever. Worship, therefore, is the fuel and goal in missions. It's the goal of mission because in mission we simply aim to bring the nations into the white-hot enjoyment of God's glory. The goal of mission is the gladness of the peoples in the greatness of God. ... Mission begins and ends in worship.'
John Piper

[*Let the Nations Be Glad: The Supremacy of God in Missions*, p11]

"The mountains and hills do not willingly worship. In all the earth, only humans have this unique capacity."
John Piper

WORSHIP

And above all these...

'I will bow down toward your holy temple and will praise your name for your love and your faithfulness, for you have exalted above all things your name and your word.'
Psalm 138:2

In addition to these four important stages, we must also assert that worship, in and of itself, is a fulfilment of the mission of God. God is working, by definition, towards the restoration of relationship with his creatures: and worship is a visible expression of relationship restored.

'The climax of God's happiness is the delight he takes in the echoes of his excellence in the praises of his people.'
John Piper
[*Desiring God*, p32]

'Worship is God's enjoyment of us and our enjoyment of him.'
Graham Kendrick
[*Worship*, p22]

As well as celebrating mission, energising mission and providing the future goal towards which mission moves, worship consummates God's mission. Communion with God is the prize that Christ has won for us, and intimacy is the lost jewel he has fought for. Worship does more than point to God's future: it brings God's future into the here and now.

'Worship is an end in itself because it is the final end for which we were created.'
John Piper
[*Desiring God*, p84]

'There are seven Greek words [for worship]: five of these occur once, another occurs three times, but the final one appears no less than fifty-nine times. This word is proskyneo... The basic meaning is 'to come towards to kiss (the hand)' and it denotes both the external act of prostrating oneself in worship and the corresponding inner attitude of reverence and humility. ... This gives us

a beautiful picture of worship as we approach the King of kings and Lord of lords; with open face, eye to eye, our hearts full of love and thanks, our wills set firmly to obey him, enjoying an intimacy and mutual affection that the watching angels find astounding.'
Graham Kendrick
[*Worship*, p23] ■

Branch Lines

BRANCH LINE
Worship and the creative arts

Exodus 35:30–36:1

The instructions for the tabernacle point towards a highly creative form of worship, drawing on a vast range of skills, crafts and resources. There is a strong emphasis on the visual, and on the physical environment, and there is recognition that the artists involved in the project are anointed ['filled with the Spirit of God' Exod 35:31] for their task. The pattern that emerges is one in which the gifts of the Creator – in terms of human skills and ingenuity and all the resources of the natural world – are brought back to God as an offering.

Over centuries Christian worship has changed in style and substance many times over. There are as many ways to worship God as there are to say, "I love you." But if the Exodus story is a source and model for us, it will drive us above all to seek creativity in worship. Worship is "all we are, responding to all God is". The tabernacle instructions point towards six reasons to maximise creativity as the heart of worship.

Creativity in worship reflects God's creativity

'Bezalel executes in miniature the divine creative role of Genesis 1 in the building of the tabernacle. The Spirit of God with which the craftsmen are filled is a sign of the living, breathing force that lies behind the completing of the project just as it lies behind the creation. Their intricate craftsmanship mirrors God's own work. The

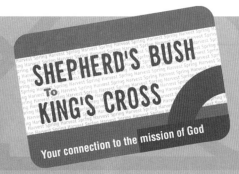
SHEPHERD'S BUSH
To
KING'S CROSS
Your connection to the mission of God

precious metals with which they work take up the very products of God's beautiful creation and give new shape to that beauty within the creation. ... The importance given to shape, order, design, intricacy – for example, the embroidery (36:37; 38:18) – and the visual aspect, including colour (36:8; 35; 38:18–23), in both structure and furnishings, corresponds with the orderly, colourful, artful, and intricate creation of Genesis 1.'
Terence E. Fretheim

[*Interpretation: Exodus*, pp269, 270]

'Creativity is what God is all about, we're made in his image. Leaders, preoccupied with the five m's – meetings, music, ministry, miracles and money – have neglected movement, colour, taste, smell and touch. We must use all means to celebrate and communicate the love God has for people and the joys and pains we experience in our struggle to know him.'
John Noble

[*The Shaking*]

Creativity in worship touches the whole person

'If we genuinely believe that salvation is for the whole person, then we must cater for the whole person in worship, allowing the truth about God to be encountered by all our senses as well as by our spirit.'
Graham Kendrick

[*Worship*, p109]

'When we are worshipping God we should do so with our whole being. That means becoming more authentically human; it means drawing out our true identities and being free to be ourselves before God and each other; ... it means celebrating all facets of our humanity, and using the full range of creativity which God has placed within us.'
Brian and Kevin Draper

[*Refreshing Worship*, p96]

Creativity in worship projects a bigger picture

Creativity worship is wide-screen: it has the power to create and celebrate a bigger picture of who God is. Stewart Henderson, the poet, has commented:

'If you banish poetry and the other expressive arts to the dim cloisters of our faith, then what takes place is in effect the banning of God thinking aloud. But there are still many who view poetry as something of which to be suspicious and to slander as irrelevant. And it is at this point that the English church, like the country outside its doors, seems to have lost its sight. Not hearing or seeing the full foaming God of the sea and the sacraments.'
['If Albion could sing again' in *Anglicans for Renewal*, Volume 58]

'The church must seek out her poets and artists, film-makers, liturgists, painters, musicians, photographers, sculptors and storytellers, recover her imagination, filling up an empty ritual to tell the story again.'
Jonny Baker

['Rhythm of the Masses' in Pete Ward Ed., *Mass Culture*, p47]

Creativity in worship enacts the sacrifice of praise

In worship we bring before God the fruits of our lives. Creativity enables us to symbolise and enact this offering.

In her studies of the Russian Orthodox church, Jenny Robertson records an interview with a painter of icons: "We paint the lives of saints, but we're concerned with something more than biography. We preach the gospel, but we use no words. Our work uses created things, wood and linen, chalk, organic materials, egg yolk, lapis lazuli, gold, linseed oil, resins, amber. We offer them back to the Creator."

[*Windows to Eternity*, p59]

John Noble describes the breadth of worship as "the dancers, film-makers, potters, weavers, poets, architects, builders, jewellers, administrators, cooks, teachers,

"How shall we honour God in worship? By saying, 'It's my duty'? Or by saying, 'It's my joy'?"
John Piper

WORSHIP

initiators, servants and many, many more bringing their skills to restore and beautify the living temple of our living God, in a fitting tribute to the one who bled and died to make this new technicoloured age of grace, creativity and everlasting joy a reality."

[*The Shaking*]

Creativity in worship offers Holy Space

'We need space – time to contemplate and meditate. In fact, time to stop is becoming a rare commodity. Even in our sleep we are processing the busyness of the day and trying to cope with it. Like the TV, it seems almost impossible to switch off. ... We can counter the culture by promoting the idea of sacred space. We can give people the time, the peace, the quiet and the reflection that they just don't get outside – the time for prayer and worship; the time to think about the things that really count.'

Brian and Kevin Draper

[*Refreshing Worship*, p25]

'There is, in fact, a tremendous hunger now in the West to rediscover holy places. Places where tragic accidents happen are quickly turned into shrines, with flowers, candles, toys, photographs of the child struck down in a car accident, of the victim of violent crime.'

Jenny Robertson

[*Windows to Eternity*, p57]

Creativity in worship connects with a visual and sensory age

'TVs, CPUs, VCRs and VDUs – not books – have become the weapons of the contemporary revolution. Control the visual media and you win the war, whether it's Serb versus Croat or Coke versus Pepsi.'

Brian and **Kevin Draper**

[*Refreshing Worship*, p36]

There is in fact a long tradition of 'visual worship' in the Christian church. Andrew Walker notes:

'We can see the different ways in which cultures have responded to Jesus in their religious iconography. The ancient Syrian church of South India, for example, presents Jesus as the guru complete with turban. Quite naturally, the Ethiopian Jesus is black, and the Russian Orthodox Christ is Russified and noticeably softer and more recognisably human than the stylised and stern Jesus of Byzantium.'

[*Telling the Story*, p19] ■

Close Up:

These examples – and many more we could cite – show how art becomes part of incarnation. Whilst words often remain detached and universal, art often brings Jesus down to earth, dressing him in local clothes. It is a way of declaring that as well as being God's only son, Jesus is also our only saviour – he belongs both to God and to us. A painting by an anonymous Korean artist illustrates this. Jesus, painted as a Korean, is shown carrying his cross, and with it a strangely shaped burden. To the foreigner the shape is a mystery: but to every Korean it is instantly recognisable as the outline of the two halves of their nation – North and South. Bitterly divided for many years, Korea is brought together, here, by the death of Jesus. The art and creativity of our worship can be used by God to bring timeless truths alive in the immediate context of our time and culture.

In Brief:

In Exodus, craftsmen were filled with the Spirit of God to make the tabernacle a place of excellence in worship. What might it mean in our day for worship to mobilise "every skilled person to whom the LORD has given skill and ability to know how to carry out all the work of constructing the sanctuary"?

[Exod 36:1]?

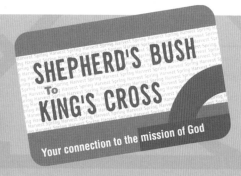

SHEPHERD'S BUSH
TO
KING'S CROSS

Your connection to the mission of God

BRANCH LINE
Worship as a
contemplative heart

The emphasis in the tabernacle passages is on corporate worship. It is together that the people of God will declare and celebrate his presence. But there is also a significant thread of individual worship running through the narrative – particularly in the life of Moses. Worship is not only what we do when we gather, it is also what we do when we're alone. Moses is an example of the person who contributes to public worship out of the strength gained in private worship: who 'comes into the presence of men and women out of the presence of God'.

'The LORD would speak to Moses face to face, as a man speaks with his friend. Then Moses would return to the camp.'

[Exod 33:11]

Christian history attests time and time again to the power and passion gained in private worship. Worship is a public festival, but it is also a private feast. It is not only central to the life of the Christian community – it is also the core of each Christian life. The tabernacle established the presence of God at the heart of his people: Pentecost establishes the presence of God in the hearts of his people.

A heart of worship is the source of our strength

'The words we use in trying to communicate the Christian message in the Christian experience have to be charged with strength and power, but they can only be charged with strength and power if they spring from the silence of the spirit in our inner being... .'
John Main

[Richard J. Foster & Emilie Griffin, *Spiritual Classics: reading with the heart*, p179]

A heart of worship is alive to awe

'G.K Chesterton once suggested that "the greatest of all illusions is the illusion of familiarity." Familiarity is also the death of respect, wonder and awe. When our minds, hearts, and imaginations are no longer poised for surprise and astonishment, when we feel that we have already understood something, then we no longer have a healthy fear of God or indeed of each other.'
Roland Rolheiser

[*The Shattered Lantern: rediscovering a felt presence of God*, p107]

A heart of worship connects with God's creation

'So, God speaks to us through the world around us. All the beauty that I see in creation must in some way be in him who made it. We should strive to think of him in new ways, we should try to break out of stereotyped manner of speaking with him. Perhaps we should address him as 'the One who makes the rainbows', or as 'the One who listens to the hills', and thus begin to form a new picture of awe and beauty to replace our dull and faded images.'
Ian Petit

[*The God Who Speaks*, p77]

Close Up:
The Celtic traditions of worship – ancient and modern – exemplify the desire to worship God in, with and through his whole creation:

'My mother would be asking us to sing our morning song to God down in the back house, as Mary's lark was singing it up in the clouds and as Christ's thrush was singing it yonder in the tree, giving glory to the God of the creatures for the repose of the night, for the light of the day and for the joy of life. She would tell us that every creature on the earth here below and in ocean beneath and in the air above was giving glory to the great God of the creatures and of the worlds, of the virtues and the blessings, and would we be dumb?'
Catherine Maclennan

[interviewed by Alexander Carmichael, *Carmina Gadelica*]

WORSHIP

A heart of worship elevates the everyday

'Birth, life, work, love, death can be regarded as a meaningless fate, or they can become free and joyful acceptance, ecstatic contemplation, a hymn to joy.'
Carlo Caretto

[*Love is for Living*, p36]

'I should like to speak of God not on the borders of life but at its centre ... God is the "beyond" in the midst of our life.'
Dietrich Bonhoeffer ■

In Brief:

Worshippers bring the whole of their lives into the presence of God – and the presence of God into the whole of their lives. By God's Spirit, they become 'multiple tabernacles', mobile homes for God. Just as God journeyed with his pilgrim people Israel, so he journeys with each believer. A heart of worship celebrates the real presence of God in the world.

Billboards

 ## FELLOW TRAVELLERS

Worship Together?

'Some years ago I visited a seaside church while on holiday. The small congregation was distributed throughout the cavernous building. I smiled at a lady nearby. She looked alarmed. Everyone else seemed to be doing their best to avoid eye-contact. We were all in the same place at the same time, and outwardly doing similar things, but there was no sense in which we were worshipping together.'
Pamela Evans

[*Building the Body*, p28]

Openings

O Lord God, Creator of all
Open my eyes to beauty
Open my mind to wonder
Open my ears to others
Open my heart to you.
David Adam

[*Power Lines*]

ESE Worship [Entire Sensory Experience]

'What is it about sitting on a surfboard beyond the breaking waves on a beautiful, clear morning that is so wonderful? It is the smell and taste of the salty sea, the sound of the pounding waves, the cry of the seagulls, the spray on your face, the cool, silky water, the warm glow of the sun, the anticipation and excitement of the next wave on the horizon, the good feeling in your body from the endorphins released by the last ride, the camaraderie of fellow surfers out there with you... . It is about an entire sensory experience. It is the engagement of the full range of senses. And so it should be with our worship?'
Brian and Kevin Draper

[*Refreshing Worship*, p96] ■

 ## APPLICATIONS

This is My Church...

Kenny Mitchell is a professional DJ who likens the contemporary tools of turntables, CD players, drum machines, samplers and computers to the ancient temple instruments of Israel. Often DJ'ing in the context of 'secular' clubs, Kenny says: "I'll be praying, 'OK God, some people here are depressed, some are on a high, some are sick. I want to see freedom and joy and something of your truth come out. You've given me two turntables and a CD player – God, do your stuff.' And he does." Kenny describes a recent club night in Osaka, Japan: "At 3:30am we were still spinning and God just moved through the music. Four people became Christians through conversations they had in the chill-out room.

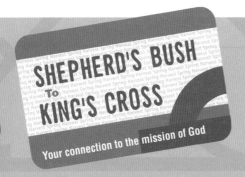

SHEPHERD'S BUSH
To
KING'S CROSS

Your connection to the mission of God

The non-believers wanted a spiritual experience, it was the Christians who were most freaked out."

- Is this a description of worship – or of mission?
- Is there a place for worship in 'secular' contexts and venues?
- How else might Christians take worship 'out of its box' and into mission?

Graceway...

Steve Taylor describes the worship of Graceway, a Baptist church in Auckland, New Zealand.

'A faith community for Xers/postmodern pilgrims/those feeling 20-30 something, that is committed to being creative and relevant, real and honest, relaxed and relational. The church community gathers every Sunday evening, starting with a provided meal, cafe style, around low tables. The meal connects people as a community and invokes an earthy, relational spirituality. Participation is essential. Children are included as much as possible. Up to eight people can take different parts of the service. Worship is widely varied and can involve the writing of prayers, the lighting of candles, a corporate dance, song, written liturgy or reflection on symbols. Strongly aware of the contemporary culture and the need to contextualise, TV advertisements, video and slides are used to introduce worship, as 'worship wallpaper' and as sites for prayer. Worship includes 'bar stool time'; a real bar stool which is open for anyone to sit on and contribute poetry, life's ups and downs, a need for prayer, a personal or family milestone. The bar stool time finishes with prayer for what was shared, for the community and world. A 'sermon' slot is retained, ten to fifteen minutes that work hard to connect with a visually orientated culture and includes interaction, discussion and visual symbols.'

[*The Rata*, unpublished paper, November 1999]

- Is this different from your experience of worship?
- Is it just for the young, or a model of how worship might change for all of us?

- What other models do you know of that adapt worship to a contemporary setting?

God in Everyday Places...

'I now see clearly that, if there is any path at all on which I can approach you, it must lead through the very middle of my ordinary daily life. If I should try to flee to you by any other way, I'd actually be leaving myself behind, and that, aside from being quite impossible, would accomplish nothing at all.'
Karl Rahner

- Is there a 'path to God' through the middle of your everyday life?
- How might such a path be discovered and maintained? ◼

 BOOK STALL

The Christ We Share published by CMS, USPG and the Methodist Church. Containing picture cards, OHP transparencies, background material and suggested exercises, this pack explores images of Jesus from around the world. An excellent resource for schools and local churches. A highly effective means of communicating the global nature of Christ's church. ◼

Pete Ward (Ed.), The Eucharist and the Mass Culture, SPCK, 1999

Lesslie Newbigin, The Household of God, Paternoster, 1998

Margaret Silf, Sacred Spaces, Lion

John Piper, Desiring God, IVP

Ronald Rolheiser, Against an Infinite Horizon

Jenny Robertson, Windows to Eternity, Bible Reading Fellowship

Jack Hayford, Worship His Majesty, Gospel Light

John Piper, Let The Nations be Glad, IVP

Brian and Kevin Draper, Refreshing Worship, Bible Reading Fellowship

Graham Kendrick, Worship, Kingsway

Matt Redman, The Unquenchable Worshipper, Kingsway

COMMUNITY

1 DESTINATIONS AND DEFINITIONS
Community

community *noun* (*communities*) **1 a** the group of people living in a particular place; **b** the place in which they live. **2** a group of people bonded together by a common religion, nationality or occupation • *the Asian community*. **3** a religious or spiritual fellowship of people living together. **4** the quality or fact of being shared or common • *community of interests*. **5** a group of states with common interests. **6** the public; society in general. **7** *biol* a naturally occurring group of different plant or animal species that occupy the same habitat and interact with each other.
ETYMOLOGY: 14c: from Latin *communitas* fellowship, from *communis* common

© Copyright Chambers Harrap Publishers Ltd 2002

Israel begins the drama as an oppressed generation of slaves, but ends it as a nation. God's acts of liberation and salvation are people-forming in their implications. Exodus is a story of community... . ■

District Lines

Exodus is first and foremost the story of Yahweh – the Creator God who reveals himself as Redeemer. In another sense it is the biography of Moses, who hears the call of God and is transformed into a spiritual, legal and political leader. But there is a third character whose origins, adventures and ultimate fate form a crucial thread in the drama: Israel.

'Exodus is the story of the rebirth of a nation, a nation that sprang miraculously from its elderly parents, Abraham and Sarah, flourished for a period in both Canaan and Egypt, and then all but disappeared under the cruel oppression of Pharaoh's rule.'
James D. Newsome
[*Exodus – Interpretation Bible Studies*, p119]

The Hebrew slaves are formed and shaped by the events of this story, becoming a community of God's people. The people of Israel are:

- **A chosen people:** Israel is defined by God's initiative and choice (in Exodus & Passover)
- **A called people:** Israel will be God's people for the sake of all people
- **A consecrated people:** Israel is called to bear the image of God in the world "carry his likeness"
- **A covenant people:** to be part of Israel is both to belong and to believe. ■

2 A CHOSEN PEOPLE
Defined by God's choice

Deuteronomy 7:7–8
In Exodus 12:3, in the build-up to the Passover, the phrase 'the whole community of Israel' is used – the first time the slaves are described in this way. It is the actions of God – in Passover and Exodus – that define the people. They are formed by God's choice.

"The nation of Israel was really formed at the Exodus," Mark Stibbe writes. "It was only when the Israelites

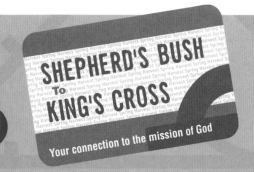

SHEPHERD'S BUSH
To
KING'S CROSS
Your connection to the mission of God

"But it is not we who build. He wills to build the church. No man builds the church but Christ alone. Whoever is minded to build the church is surely well on the way to destroying it; for he will build a temple to idols without wishing or knowing it. We must confess – He builds. We must proclaim – He builds. We must pray to him – He builds."
Dietrich Bonhoeffer

came out from under the oppression of the Egyptians that they became a separate people. It is only when they were given the commandments at Mount Sinai that they received the divine instructions that would enable them to develop their own distinctive identity as a nation. From this point onwards, the people of Israel enjoyed a special status as God's adopted son."

[*From Orphans to Heirs*, p36]

'Prior to the exodus from Egypt, the Bible tells us of God's call to individuals and to families. But the phrase 'the people of Israel' is first used in Exodus. The descendants of these same individuals and families are now fused into a people and a community by the founding acts of liberation and covenant.'

Os Guinness

[*The Call*, p101] ■

A CALLED PEOPLE
God's people for the sake of all people

Deuteronomy 4:6–8

Israel does not only have an identity because of God's mercy: they also have a calling and a purpose. They are to be God's people for the sake of all people, a holy nation for the sake of the nations. The most consistent definition of the people of God in both Old and New Testaments is 'the called out ones'. Israel, and later the church, is a community of those who have responded to the call of God.

'Our word church translates the common, secular Greek word for a popular 'assembly'. But with its root meaning in the word for 'called out' and its Old Testament meaning in the idea of a 'called out people', the church is the assembly of God's people, called out by him and belonging to him.'

Os Guinness

[*The Call*, p101]

'Israel is called because the whole earth belongs to Yahweh. His people, who are set apart to serve him as a holy God, are to mediate his presence and blessings to the surrounding nations.'

Andreas J. Köstenberger & Peter T. O'Brien

[*Salvation to the Ends of the Earth*, p252] ■

Close Up:

'The calling of Israel to bear faithful witness to the revelation of the living God entrusted to them was not a matter of Israel's flaunting their privilege in an attitude of 'our religion is better than yours' – as if Israel's faith was one among many brands of a commodity, 'human religion.' Rather, what was at stake, what was so threatened by Israel compromising with the gods and worship of other nations, was the continuity of the redemptive work of the Creator God of all mankind within the unique historical and social context which he himself had chosen.'

Vinoth Ramachandra

[*Faiths in Conflict?*, p97]

In Brief:

'God created the people known as Israel for one purpose, to be the servants of Jehovah until through them every nation came to know who Jehovah was.'

Oswald Chambers

[*So I Send You*, p92]

A CONSECRATED PEOPLE
Imaging God in the world

Deuteronomy 28:9–10

The 'means' by which Israel would make Yahweh known among the nations would be through reflecting his character in their national life.

"One of my favourite activities while preaching is to look the congregation straight in the eye and say, 'The greatest sin of the church today is not any sin of commission or sin of omission, but the sin of...' At this point I hesitate, waiting for someone to finish the sentence. Never has someone not spoken the words, 'No mission.'"

Leonard Sweet

COMMUNITY

'Israel is to be holy – its special relationship to God makes Israel set apart from other nations. ... Israel is to be morally consistent, embracing the foundational values of justice and compassion, just as those values are embraced by Israel's holy God.'
James D Newsome
[Interpretation Bible Studies: Exodus, p69]

'God's activity becomes a paradigm for Israel; its life is to be lived in imitation of God. As God was compassionate toward the oppressed, so is Israel to be compassionate. As God truly entered into the suffering of the people and made it his own, so also is Israel to engage in an internal relationship with those who suffer.'
Terence E Fretheim
[Interpretation: Exodus, p61]

In Brief:
The more Israel came to know and worship God, the more like him they would become: until they could genuinely be said to 'carry his likeness' in the world. Their calling was to become 'the image of God'.

'It is a law of life that we become like those we constantly gaze at. The eye exercises a great influence on life and character. The education of a child is conducted largely through the eye. He is moulded by the manners and habits of those he constantly sees.'
J Oswald Sanders
[Spiritual Maturity] ■

A COVENANT PEOPLE
Belonging and believing

Exodus 19:5
The basis of Israel's security is God's covenant – his commitment to them. They belong to him because he has chosen it so. But the covenant is reciprocal – from a position of belonging, they are invited to believe. Through worship, instruction and the leadership of

Moses, the people will enter in more and more fully to their identity. The phrase 'people of God' comes to represent a statement both of belonging and of believing.

James D Newsome writes: "God's salvation of Israel is a reciprocal or covenantal relationship, one in which the people express their acceptance of God's love by certain patterns of worship and of interaction with one another."
[Interpretation Bible Studies: Exodus, p3] ■

Close Up
In describing the Exodus event as "the Easter event of the Old Testament", Newsome suggests the four stages of covenant that culminate in a people who both belong to God (by his choice) and believe in him (by theirs):
'Easter and Exodus is an apt comparison for at least these reasons:
By means of God's miraculous power, people are saved from an evil before which they are powerless.
As a result, those who have been saved enter into a new dimension of their relationship with God, a new covenant or, to be more precise, a reformulation of an existing covenant.
In spite of their continued sinfulness, God clings to this freshly covenanted community and they to God.
In their joyful acceptance of God's initiatives, the saved people assume new understandings of the trust placed in them as God's covenant people.'
[Interpretation Bible Studies: Exodus, p1]

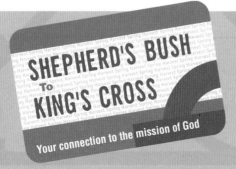

SHEPHERD'S BUSH
to
KING'S CROSS
Your connection to the mission of God

"I understand Christian witness to include the declaration of the gospel by life, word and deed. By life I refer to the fact that Christians are the message. We are the sixty-seventh book of the Bible. People read our lives, our actions and our words and believe that they know what being a Christian means."
Bryant L Myers

In Brief:

Chosen by God, for the sake of the nations, to bear his image in the world through belonging and believing: these are the foundational parameters of the community of God revealed in the Exodus narrative. Equally, these are the realities:

- Ultimately fulfilled in Jesus, God's chosen servant, who embodies in his own life and death the vocation of Israel.
- Definitive of the Christian church, God's redeemed community and the body of Christ on earth.

Main Lines

MAIN LINE
Community and the mission of God

Just as the mission of God formed the people of the Exodus, so the New Testament church is formed as the mission of God finds fulfilment. Like the white water churned up in the wake of an ocean liner, the church comes into being where the mission of God is. The same four characteristics that were true of the Exodus-formed people of Israel are true, now, of Christ's church.

The church is defined by God's choice

The Passover and the Exodus were formative events for the people of Israel. God's choices, actions and initiative created the context in which it was possible for Israel to become 'the people of God'. Their very identity was a response to his choice. In the same way the church is called into being by the choices God has made. The incarnation, death and resurrection of Jesus resound through history as once-for-all God events. The church is the community of those who respond.

'The church, as the corporate body of believers, is a result of the message of Jesus. It is an outgrowth of the mission of God through Christ. ... The church, then, should conceive of itself as the "outcome of the activity of God who sends and saves".'
Gailyn Van Rheenen
[*Missions: Biblical Foundations and Contemporary Strategies*, p25]

This means:

The church is the result of God's mission, but not its focus

'In speaking of evangelism, one must speak of church growth, but only at the end of the dramatic process, and not any sooner. Evangelism is never aimed at institutional enhancement or aggrandisement. It is aimed simply and solely at summoning people to new, liberated obedience to the true governor of all created reality. The church is a modest gathering locus for those serious about the new governance. There must be such a gathering and such a meeting, and such a community, because the new governance is inherently against autonomy, isolation, and individualism. The church grows because more and more persons change allegiance, switch worlds, accept the new governance and agree to the unending and difficult task of appropriating the news in practical ways.'
Walter Brueggemann
[*Perspectives on Evangelism*, p45]

'The church's final word is not "church" but the glory of the Father and the Son in the spirit of liberty.'
Jurgen Moltmann
[*The Church in the Power of the Spirit*, p19]

Community is an essential ingredient in God's plan

'The call of Jesus is personal but not purely individual; Jesus summons his followers not only to an individual calling but also to a corporate calling.'
Os Guinness
[*The Call*, p98]

"A prominent Hindu once said that he would believe in the Christian Saviour if Christians only looked a little more saved."
Church of Scotland
[A Church Without Walls p9]

COMMUNITY

'The fellowship of Jesus' followers is not merely a loose coalition of individuals who acknowledge Jesus… Rather, it is a community of disciples who seek to walk together in accordance with the principles of the kingdom.'
Stanley J Grenz

[*Theology for the Community of God*, p656]

In Brief:

'It is not that the church 'has' a mission, but the very reverse: the mission of Christ creates his own church.'
Church of Scotland

[*A Church Without Walls*, p10]

The church is God's people for the sake of all people

Just as the people of Israel were chosen 'for the sake of the nations', so the church lives not for itself but for others.

'The church is the church only when it exists for others.'
Dietrich Bonhoeffer

It follows that the church can only truly be itself when it embraces a full participation in God's mission. A church that hears the offer of salvation but is deaf to the call to service is not in any true or effective sense the community of God.

'The church's existence is in the act of being the bearer of salvation to the whole world. … It is true to its own essential nature only when it takes this fact seriously and therefore treats the world-wide mission of the church as something which belongs to the very core of its existence as a corporate body.'
Lesslie Newbigin

'Mission is the very lifeblood of the church. As the body cannot survive without blood, so the church cannot survive without mission. Without blood the body dies; without mission the church dies. As the physical body becomes weak without sufficient oxygen-carrying red blood cells, so the church becomes anaemic if it does not express its faith. The church … establishes its rationale for being – its purpose for existing – while articulating its faith. An unexpressed faith withers. A Christian fellowship without mission loses its vitality. Mission is the force that gives the body of Christ vibrancy, purpose, and direction. When the church neglects its role as God's agent for mission, it is actually neglecting its own lifeblood.'
Gailyn Van Rheenen

[*Missions: Biblical Foundations and Contemporary Strategies*, p31]

'Mission work does not arise from any arrogance in the Christian church: mission is its cause and its life. The church exists by mission, just as fire exists by burning.'
Emil Brunner

It is not just that the church is a useful tool in the fulfilment of God's mission: it's his chosen vehicle of self-expression. A redeemed community declaring and demonstrating the victory of God in Christ is not just one possible means of winning the world. It is, by God's decision, the one, only and best means.

'How is it possible that the gospel should be credible, that people should come to believe that the power which has the last word in human affairs is represented by a man hanging on a cross? I'm suggesting that the only answer, the only hermeneutic of the gospel, is a congregation of men and women who believe it and live by it.'
Lesslie Newbigin

In Brief:

The church – the assembly of the called-out ones – is God's chosen vehicle for his mission to the world. There is no 'Plan B'.

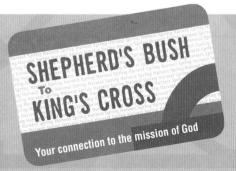

SHEPHERD'S BUSH
to
KING'S CROSS
Your connection to the mission of God

"When you can put your church on the back of a camel, then I will believe Christianity is for us."
Somali camel herder

The church bears the image of God in the world

Israel was called, through gazing on God in worship, to be transformed into his likeness – to bear his image in the earth. In the same way Christ's church is called to carry the mark of its Saviour, bearing the image of the crucified King. The church does not proceed in power but in weakness; it does not seek to conquer so much as to convert; it makes no man or woman a slave and is the servant of all. The true calling of the church is to be the community of the Christ-like.

'Jesus broke down social barriers in forming around himself an alternative community drawn from the marginalized peoples of Palestinian society. What the Pharisees saw as sinful disregard of covenant ideals, Jesus saw as the birth of a new covenant, the visible expression of God's liberating reign. In the table-fellowship that he and his disciples celebrated, and to which the 'tax-collectors and sinners' were invited unconditionally, Jesus was enacting a parable. Here was a foretaste of the messianic banquet, when "many will come from the east and the west, and will take their places at the feast with Abraham, Isaac and Jacob in the kingdom of heaven"'.
Vinoth Ramachandra
[*Faiths in Conflict?*, p101]

'We are here and we are joined together not as a community of those who know, but of those who all look for the word of their Lord and seek everywhere if they cannot hear it, not as those who know, but as those who seek, those who are hungry, those who wait, those who are in need, those who hope.'
Dietrich Bonhoeffer
[*No Rusty Swords*, p181]

Close Up:

'The ripping of the temple curtain in two (Mark 15:38) graphically underlines what his selection of disciples exemplifies. The cross has made access to God available to all, irrespective of gender or race. The old "private access" road of Judaism has been closed. There is only one access route in the new age, and it goes through the cross. And along that way tread men and women, Jews and Gentiles, black and white, rich and poor, all on a level footing, carrying their own crosses, enjoying restored communion with God and forming the new humanity.'
Derek Tidball
[*The Message of the Cross*, p150]

In Brief:

As the people of Israel were called to be distinct from the nations around them: to carry a different DNA, so the Christian community is not to be like other communities. It is to be ruled by a different standard: just and loving, and open to all.

The church is founded on both belonging and believing

Membership of this new community, the church, is not simply a question of beliefs – it is also an expression of belonging. The church is God's new covenant community, the family that bears his name. 'Belonging without believing' (nominalism) and 'believing without belonging' (individualism) are both expressions of an incomplete faith. They may be stages on a journey of faith, but the full picture of covenantal love is only seen when both are present. To believe is to enter into belonging: new birth is birth into family.

COMMUNITY

"The way of grace," the Church of Scotland report *A Church Without Walls* suggests, "is to give people a place of belonging, leading to opportunities of believing and then exploring patterns of Christ-like behaviour."

[*A Church Without Walls*, p24]

'In the New Testament, it is not so much that there are different churches in different places as that there is one church in many places.'
Os Guinness
[*The Call*, p101]

Close Up:

'All those in whom Christ dwells through faith, all who have been accepted by God in Christ, are now family members. The Christian thus has a double nationality: his own former loyalty to biological family, tribe, clan or nation is retained, but is now set within a wider and more demanding loyalty to the global family of Christ. The new adopted family stretches back in time as well as outward in space. It spans generations as well as cultures and nations. It reaches back to Abraham and to the faithful since Abraham, so that every new convert now finds his or her history drawn into the history of Israel in the Hebrew Bible and that of the people of God of the New Testament age (Rom 4:11–12; Heb 11: 39–40). What this means is that, for me as an Asian Christian, Augustine and Irenaeus, Teresa of Avila and Mary Slessor, Calvin and Bonhoeffer all become my ancestors, part of my personal family tree. And, for Western Christians their family tree now includes John of Damascus, Panditha Ramabai, Sadhu Sundar Singh, Kagawa and a host of outstanding Asian Christian men and women. I often wonder what a revolution this simple gospel concept would cause in Western theological education if grasped and applied in the curriculum!'
Vinoth Ramachandra
[*Faiths in Conflict*, p101]

In Brief:

In a world of conflict and fragmentation, searching in vain for a common language of humanity, the 'distributed body' of Christ is a symbol of the new life possible in God.

'In the postmodern period we can expect a new interest to emerge in the visible church, both local and universal. The local church will increasingly work toward an experienced community of faith, a community that has historical continuity with two thousand years of history, a community that is related to the global church. Once again, the church in society will seek to be the incarnate presence of God in tangible form.'
Robert Webber
[*Ancient-Future Faith*, p75] ∎

MAIN LINE
No more idols

'Put away the gods of your ancestors beyond the River and in Egypt [Josh 24:14]. Remove, get rid of other gods. There can be no other loyalties if the story of Yahweh is embraced. This demand is a deep either/or that touches every aspect of life, personal and social, intimate and public.'
Walter Brueggemann
[*Perspectives on Evangelism*, p63]

There is one family, one new humanity; distributed through time and space and proclaiming by its very life the miracle that community is possible.

The commitment of the Hebrew slaves to 'be God's people' – their part in the covenant agreement – was often expressed in negative terms: they were to turn away from belonging to other gods. God's claim on the new community was exclusive: there was no place for idols.

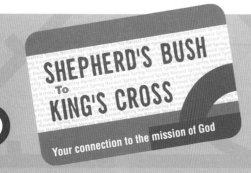

SHEPHERD'S BUSH
to
KING'S CROSS
Your connection to the mission of God

"Just the thought of Eddie Izzard makes me smile. I like what he says about Christianity, that somehow we've managed to transform it from Jesus' model of 'hang out and be groovy' into the church's 'mumbling in cold buildings'."
David Westlake
[*Upwardly Mobile: How to Live a Life of Significance*, p8]

Close Up:

The claim of the Old Testament is that those who worship idols become like them. Just as God's chosen community, when they are faithful to his covenant, reflect his image in the world, so idolaters create lives and societies in the image of their idols. Christian economist Bob Goudzwaard suggests that this is still the case, formulating three basic 'rules' of the impact of idolatry on our lives:

- Everyone serves god(s) in their lives
- Everyone is transformed into an image of their god
- Mankind creates and forms a structure of society in its own image and, hence, into the image of its idols.

[Cited in Paul Marshall, *Thine is the Kingdom*]

It is for this reason that idols are so often associated with success and power. "When the Israelites entered Canaan", Chris Wright suggests, "they were surrounded by a culture that was successful by the standards of that time. Canaanite civilisation might have been morally degenerate but its progress in agriculture, urbanisation and literacy was excellent. It was a prosperous international civilisation. And Baal was its god. Baal was the god of money, of the land, of business, of fertility, of sex; he was the god of everything that mattered. So it might have seemed a good idea, in addition to worshipping Yahweh, to get on the right side of Baal and certain other gods."

[*Ambassadors to the World*, p56]

'Idolatry. ... is the great enemy of God's people, and the great threat to their witness to the nations. The nations already follow their own gods. So if we, the people chosen to bring the knowledge of the living God to the nations, go after their gods, there will be no difference between us and them, and no witness, no message, no mission.'

Chris Wright

[*Ambassadors to the World*, pp23–24]

"When we think of idolatry, we tend to think of strange practices in foreign countries, strange and horrible things we would never do ourselves," Chris Wright explains. "But our idolatry concerns the things that 'do' attract us, that dazzle our sensibilities."

[*Ambassadors to the World*, p25]

Paul Marshall suggests that an idol is "a thing which human beings create or find and which they then trust in. The worshipping of idols is never a purely formal matter, like having a little shrine in the living room. Such worship is, like all worship, an act of one's life. Idolatry is

serving something other than God, it is putting our final trust in anything within the creation."

[*Thine is the Kingdom*]

In our own day, Tom and Christine Sine ask: "Where are we likely to find the good life for ourselves and those we care about? If the skyline of that land of milk and honey suddenly appeared over the next horizon would we even recognise it? Or could we be taken in by some very seductive, glittering counterfeits and take the wrong exit?"

[*Living on Purpose: Finding God's best for your life*, p15]

COMMUNITY

Close Up:

What are the idols of our time? Suggestions abound, but a number of key themes do emerge. Richard Foster suggests that contemporary idolatry is associated, more often than not, with money, sex and power and Bryant L Myers puts science, technology and capitalism in the dock, claiming that these three "continue to demand our faith and allegiance, claiming to be the only remaining story. They are gods that we are often too quick to worship."

[*Walking with the Poor*, p21]

In Brief:

Whatever the idols that vie for our allegiance, Yahweh makes his claim to exclusive ownership. We belong to him because he has chosen and saved us. We believe in him because he has proved himself to us. We are his and the contract is exclusive. He alone is worthy of our love.

'God alone needs nothing outside himself, because he himself is the highest and the only lasting good. So all objects we desire short of God are as finite and incomplete as we ourselves are and, therefore, disappointing if we make them the objects of ultimate desire.'
Os Guinness
[*The Call*, p13] ■

Branch Lines

BRANCH LINE
Owning up to our past

If our belonging to the covenant community of God makes us one with believers from every place and age, then we will be forced to accept a poor record. There are high spots of brilliant light in the history of the church, but there are also deep lines of shadow.

Close Up:

In *Service of All the Dead*, Colin Dexter's fictional detective, Inspector Morse, reflects on the sorry history of corruption in the church:

'His favourite Gibbon quotation flashed across his mind, the one concerning the fifteenth-century Pope John XXIII, which had so impressed him as a boy and which he had committed to memory those many years ago: "The most scandalous charges were suppressed: the vicar of Christ was only accused of piracy, murder, rape, sodomy, and incest." It was no new thing to realise that the Christian church had a great deal to answer for, with so much blood on the hands of its temporal administrators, and so much hatred and bitterness in the hearts of its spiritual lords. But, behind it all, as Morse knew – and transcending it all – stood the simple, historical, unpalatable figure of its founder – an enigma with which Morse's mind had wrestled so earnestly as a youth, and which even now troubled his pervasive scepticism.'
Colin Dexter
[*Service of All the Dead* (London: Pan, 1980), p.250]

"Let us be honest," Gregory Boyd urges. "The church has always been a very human and a very fallen institution, exhibiting all the carnality, pettiness, narrowness, self-centredness and abusive power tendencies that characterise all other fallen human institutions. On the

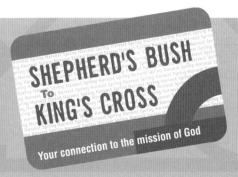

"Wretch though I be, I am the hand and foot of Christ. I move my hand and it is wholly Christ's hand. I move my foot and it is aglow with God."
St Symeon the New Theologian
(AD949–1022)

Close Up:

Whilst the mission of God always brings life and freedom, the mission of the church has too often brought death and oppression. The cases in more recent years prove that these are not out-of-date concerns.

The Anglican Church of Canada has faced bankruptcy after huge compensation claims arising from its former treatment of orphans and other children in its care.

The Irish Christian Brothers teaching order have recently apologised publicly to the generations of boys traumatised over the years by physical abuse and inappropriately violent punishments.

The Roman Catholic Church in the USA is facing the deepest crisis in its history with a huge number of accusations of sexual abuse being made against serving priests – leading to compensation claims worth tens of millions and widespread claims of a high-level cover-up.

A number of evangelical churches and high-profile ministries have faced significant public scrutiny following sexual, financial and other scandals involving figurehead leaders.

Add to these the cases of individual Christians and their leaders, and it is not difficult to see why so many people find it hard to trust the church. "What we need to do," pleads Miroslav Volf, "is to wash the face of Jesus, that beautiful face that has been dirtied by so many compromises our churches have made with the culture through the centuries."

[Cited in Dewi Hughes and Matthew Bennett, *God of the Poor*]

surface we hardly look like trophies God would want to showcase."

[*God at War*, p252]

'Happily, most people know at least some followers of Christ whose lives express the spirit of Christ and attract people to Christ. But sadly, the story of the church as a whole is the story of frequent lapses from the pattern of Christ and periods when "Christianity" was an open advertisement for the Christian view of evil rather than for Christ.'

Os Guinness

[*The Call*, p107]

Where the 'sins of our fathers' still cast their shadow over our lives and mission, we have no option but to own up, to repent and to move forward with a fresh vision of a church centred on Christ. But we may need to develop patience, understanding and a sympathetic

listening ear as more and more people cry foul and reject our community. ■

In Brief:

'The best argument for Christianity is Christians; their joy, their certainty, their completeness. But the strongest argument against Christianity is also Christians – when they are sombre and joyless, when they are self-righteous and smug in complacent consecration, when they are narrow and repressive, then Christianity dies a thousand deaths.'

Sheldon Vanauken

[Cited in Leonard Sweet, *Carpe Manana*]

COMMUNITY

BRANCH LINE
Community in community

For the mission-minded believer the call to community is not a onesided call. It is double-barrelled. We are at one and the same time called to love and serve the 'community' of the faithful – and to love and serve the wider 'community' in which it sits. We are called to be community-in-community.

Jesus said, "As the Father has sent me, I am sending you" (John 20:21). Our commission is to embody, to incarnate, Jesus in the communities where we live, work and worship.

Fran Beckett

[*Called to Action*, p76]

Being community-in-community is not easy – but several key steps help towards the goal:

Seek to be kingdom-centred, not church-absorbed

'Kingdom people seek first the kingdom of God and its justice; church people often put church work above concerns of justice, mercy and truth. Church people think about how to get people into the church; kingdom people think about how to get the church into the world. Church people worry that the world might change the church; kingdom people work to see the church change the world.'

Howard Snyder

[*Liberating the Church*, p11]

Put the goals of the kingdom first – before the institutional needs of your church. Establish personal 'kingdom priorities' and let these influence the hard choices you have to make about your time, your money and your energy levels.

Seek genuine points of contact with the wider community

'No worthwhile evangelism ever takes place in a vacuum, and few disciples will be made by a church alienated from the community in which it is set.'

George Carey

[*I Believe*, p143]

'There is nothing that generates a heart for mission more than constant contact with non-Christian realities. We cannot expect mission to happen in a church that is cut off from people outside its own culture and community.'

Andrew Lord

[*Spirit, Kingdom and Mission*, p6]

Seek to develop an in-but-not-of understanding

'The essential teaching of the early church regarding how Christians live in the world is captured in this threefold tension:
the church is separate from the world;
the church is nevertheless identified with the world;
the church seeks to transform the world.'

Robert Webber

[*Ancient-Future Faith*, p168]

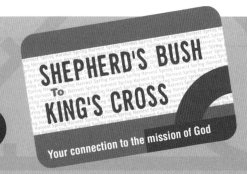

SHEPHERD'S BUSH To KING'S CROSS

Your connection to the mission of God

Close Up:

'An unfortunate legacy of pietism in the Christian church is that of regarding the world we live in as a basically hostile place and that the Christian should have no truck with the ungodly and unrighteous. This, of course, sets up battle stations at once and demarcates the battlegrounds between the church and the world. I hope that we have moved a long way from that kind of world-view, which considers our society to be utterly evil and tainted with wrong. I hope that we shall be able to enter our ministries affirming the very real experiences of grace that are found in the world and the joy which can be discovered in human gifts and beauty.'

George Carey

[*I Believe*, p30]

Seek to 'be church' whether you are gathered or dispersed

'Christians need a good theological education even more to work in a secular organisation than to work in a church. Precisely because the world-view of the secular organisation may be so fundamentally opposed to Christianity, the daily challenge of working through the variety of issues and problems may take a great deal of discernment.'

Mark Greene

[*Thank God It's Monday*, p19] ■

FELLOW TRAVELLERS

A community beetle-drive

'In 1984 people who lived in council flats in Liverpool had a problem with cockroaches. Week after week they asked the City Council to deal with the insects, but they were ignored. Finally they decided to take action. They organised a competition to see who had the biggest cockroaches. They all collected them in coffee jars and brought them to the Council Chamber to be judged. In the middle of a debate, the people let out their huge cockroaches and asked the mayor to judge whose was the biggest. The councillors were very angry, and the people were expelled from the chamber. But next day, men came round to clean up the flats!'

Roger Bowen

[*So I Send You: A Study Guide to Mission*, p200]

Building community

Eat and drink together;
Talk and laugh together;
Enjoy life together:
But never call it friendship,
Until you have wept together.

African Proverb

[*Exploring Sudanese Christianity*, CMS, 2000] ■

 ## APPLICATIONS

Believing without belonging?

The Church of Scotland report *A Church Without Walls* suggests:

'There are many Christian people who are still committed to following Jesus, but they will not or cannot express that commitment within the context of the local church. This is not the fall-out of individualism and consumerism. Quite the opposite is true. These are people in search of authentic community.'

[*A Church Without Walls*, p22]

This seems to support the claim made by Mike Riddell and others that 'the fastest growing sector of the church in the West is made up of people who don't go any more.' John Drane adds that many people influenced by the New Age movement and associated spiritualities are rejecting church – not because it is too spiritual, but because isn't spiritual enough.

- Is 'believing without belonging' an authentic way to follow Christ?
- What should we say to people who want our God but don't want our company?

COMMUNITY

● How can we reach those for whom spirituality is an individual quest and church is a cold and irrelevant institution?

Idols: Serving at the Shrine of Mammon

Ravi Zacharias quotes a newspaper report that illustrates the distortions that serving at the shrine of money can bring:

'I recall reading, in one of New York's leading newspapers, an interview with the wife of a New York Yankee ballplayer who had just signed an $89-million contract. He had held out for a long while before signing, hoping that the management would match the $91-million offer of another team. The Yankees did not budge. His wife later said, "When I saw him walk in the house, I immediately knew that he had not succeeded in persuading them to move up from eighty-nine to ninety-one million. He felt so rejected. It was one of the saddest days of our lives.'

[*Jesus Among Other Gods*, p43]

Is this kind of thinking exclusive to the rich, or are others of us guilty, but on a smaller scale?

How can we avoid letting money become our God?

Throwing the Net Wide

A challenge we face in the twenty-first century that the children of Israel didn't is the growth of the internet. Former US President Bill Clinton said recently at the London School of Economics:

'When I became president in January, 1993, there were only fifty sites on the World Wide Web. When I left office eight years later, there were 350 million.'

Web enthusiasts hail the internet as the greatest step forward in human community in centuries. Detractors say that it destroys, rather than builds, relationships, and is the enemy of true community. Christians, in the meantime, cannot decide whether 'web church' is real or fake, whether virtual worship counts and whether on-line communities are off-limits for the church. The sites below are attempts to create real worship, genuine community or Christian interaction on the web:

www.holyspace.org   www.embody.co.uk
www.theconfessor.co.uk   www.jesuit.ie/prayer
www.vurch.com   www.godweb.org

What do you think? ■

CONNECTIONS
The Simpsons
(Twentieth Century Fox)

Summary

Marge and Lisa

Marge does her best to make sure her family has some standing in the community. She is particularly keen for them to attend church – or at least for them to be seen going to church whether or not they receive anything from the experience.

Surely many mothers can identify with Marge and her attempts to hold her family together. One of Marge's aims for a respectable family lifestyle is that they should go to church. Is this what worship is all about? What does the Bible say about Marge's approach?

Lisa is determined to prove that she can get good grades at school. She is passionate about being fair and is the driving force behind the campaign to save the snakes of Springfield from being beaten to death on Whacking Day.

Lisa's sense of right and wrong is very strong, and she applies this to her spiritual outlook as well. She often

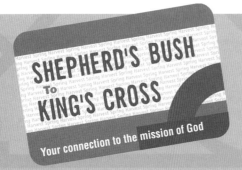

SHEPHERD'S BUSH
To
KING'S CROSS
Your connection to the mission of God

tries to influence her family to do what she sees as the right thing. This all sounds good, but what does the Bible say? Would it support her longing for order in life and religion? Does Lisa understand worship?

Bible Study

1. Marge's Weakness
– longing for respectability

'It doesn't matter how you feel inside, you know. It's what shows up on the surface that counts. Take all your bad feelings and push them down, all the way down, past your knees, until you're almost walking on them. And then you'll fit in, and you'll be invited to parties, and boys will like you ... and happiness will follow.'
(Marge)

- Read Mark 12:38–44. What motivated the Pharisees? What does Jesus see as important?
- Read Revelation 3:1–6. What was wrong with the reputation of the church in Sardis? Why is Jesus' solution appropriate?

2. Lisa's Spiritual Outlook
– wants everything in order

'I heard you last night, Bart. You prayed for this. Now your prayers have been answered ... and you owe him big.' (Lisa)

- Read 1 Corinthians 14:26–40. Why is orderly worship necessary? How does Paul expand this principle?

   Note: In the culture Paul was addressing, women were downtrodden and deemed inferior. Through the gospel, women had significant freedom. Paul is asking that women should not disrupt services by misusing their new freedom and asking numerous questions. It is Paul's belief that women should have the opportunity to learn that is so shocking here, not his

instruction for women to be quiet in church. This was revolutionary in Corinthian culture.

- Read Hebrews 10:1–25. The Jewish sacrificial system was extremely ordered. Why does the writer say that it was not the be all and end all in a relationship with God? How does Jesus supersede the system?

Implications

'I don't get it. Straight 'A's, perfect attendance, Bathroom Timer ... I should be the most popular girl in school.' (Lisa)

- Are you motivated to do things at church by what others may think of you? How can you change this?
- What is the difference between helpful order and restrictive rules in our spiritual and church lives? What does God want?

From *Connect Bible Studies: What does the Bible say about... The Simpsons.* ISBN 1 85999 529 2 published online by Damaris, and in print by Scripture Union – Linking the Word to the World. www.connectbiblestudies.com – these studies are available to buy from this site. ■

 ## THE BOOK STALL

John Drane, Cultural Change and Biblical Faith, Paternoster, 2000

Robert Webber, Ancient Future Faith, Baker

Mike Riddell, Mark Pierson, Cathy Kirkpatrick, The Prodigal Project, SPCK, 2000

Richard Tiplady, Ed., Postmission, Authentic, 2002

Michael Nazir-Ali, Shapes of the Church to Come, Kingsway

Leonard Sweet, Carpe Manana, Zondervan

Pamela Evans, Building the Body, Bible Reading Fellowship